WITHDRAWN

SYSTEMS ANALYSIS
FOR
EFFECTIVE
SCHOOL ADMINISTRATION

SYSTEMS ANALYSIS
FOR
EFFECTIVE
SCHOOL ADMINISTRATION

John McManama

Parker Publishing Company, Inc.   *West Nyack, N.Y.*

PRINTED IN THE UNITED STATES OF AMERICA
ISBN-0-13-881318-3
B&P

THE BENEFITS OF THIS BOOK

The systems approach is a powerful new tool available to school administrators for solving problems of school management. There are three operations which must be performed in a complete systems approach:

I. Analyze what needs to be done.
II. Design how it is to be done.
III. Manage the system.

This book will examine many techniques such as program budgeting and PERT scheduling as they can be utilized in schools. They will be seen in their proper context as management tools, in fact a rather minor aspect of a total systems approach.

The major thrust of this book is directed to writing performance objectives, designing systems which relate methods of production to the objectives, and managing the system by a process of evaluation which includes detection and correction of deviations from the objectives. This is what "accountability" and "management by objectives" are all about; management of the complete system including all of its interrelationships.

The modern school administrator cannot afford to be uninformed concerning the operations of systems analysis. The federal government has been insisting that more and more of its departments adopt a systems approach in their planning and budgeting. In one of his education messages, President Nixon stated, "From these considerations we derive another new concept: accountability. School administrators and school teachers alike are responsible for their performance, and it is in the interests of their pupils that they be held accountable." The major function of this book is to provide school administrators with the information needed to analyze, design, and manage a system.

A School Administrator Looks at the Systems Approach

Most of the material which has been written to date in this field has been written by systems analysts for educators. Although their understanding of systems is authoritative, they often leave the school administrator bewildered. What they lack is a clear understanding of the problems and objectives of education.

This book is written by a school administrator and is only concerned with those aspects of systems analysis which have practical application in schools. The emphasis is on educational objectives and the focus is on learning programs. The school administrator who can analyze with these principles in mind will not be easily boxed into a system which ignores the aims of the educational program.

Contents

A practical handbook on the systems approach cannot avoid an analysis of the theory on which the approach is based. It is especially important that the manager of the system, in this case the school administrator, should understand system theory. This is attended to in the first two chapters.

Chapter One gets immediately to the task of proceeding step by step through the first two operations of a systems approach. As often as possible the procedure is related to school problems. When this chapter is understood, the basic fundamentals of systems analysis and systems design will have been mastered.

"Managing the System" is the title and content matter of Chapter Two. An understanding of systems management is mandatory for the school administrator in his role as manager of the system. A straightforward explanation of cybernetics, automation, and systems theory is presented in order to equip the administrator to understand how a system works and why it is so effective. In addition, PERT scheduling is explained and illustrated.

Since the major business of schools is instruction, four chapters of this book are devoted to instructional systems. Chapter Three is devoted to those aspects of an instructional system which are usually the most difficult to work with; formulating the goal, conceptualizing the structure, selecting the process, and monitoring the system for effective operation. These are the tasks which are most often neglected and this analysis indicates how they can be performed effectively.

In order to present in detail the three operations which must be performed in a complete system, each of the next three chapters concentrates on one operation. The first operation, analyze what needs to be done, is developed in Chapter Four, "Applying an Instructional System to Elementary School Mathematics." Each of the separate tasks of this operation are followed step by step until the goals of elementary math are formulated and performance objectives are specified.

Chapter Five continues the systems approach through operation two, design the system. Individualized instruction is the area of concern in this chapter in which the solution strategy is selected and the methods of operation are outlined.

The third operation, operate the system, is developed in Chapter Six, "Organizing a Learning Disabilities Program." The aspects which must be considered in setting up management control are analyzed in sequential order. This chapter presents the details of organizing information about children with learning disabilities in such a manner that pertinent information is regularly fed back to the evaluator for processing. The implications of these techniques to other curricular areas should be apparent.

Program budgeting is probably the most frequently cited and least understood management technique which utilizes a systems approach. Chapter Seven is devoted completely to this topic. A program budget is presented as an effective technique for comparing alternative projects in terms of cost effectiveness. Many misconceptions have occurred concerning program budgets and these are considered and clarified. Most administrators approach a program budget as they would a traditional budget and quickly get bogged down in a complex network. This chapter emphasizes the purpose of program budgets as planning rather than accounting and several practical examples make this difference apparent.

"Avoiding the Systems Trap," the final chapter, presents the concerns and cautions involved when systems approaches are applied to educational problems. School administrators must be alert to the dangers and pitfalls of these techniques as well as their benefits. The effectiveness of the systems approach appeals to the cost-conscious public and unfortunately the programs which are most difficult to validate in terms of performance are usually the ones which deal with affective outcomes, process goals, and non-didactic teaching. There are some definite positions which school administrators must take to fortify their role as managers of the system. The systems approach can be a powerful ally or a dangerous adversary depending upon who is in control. The major purpose of this book is to equip school administrators to understand and perform their role as managers of the system.

To summarize: Using the information presented in this book, the school administrator should be able to:

- Write organizational goals, administrative regulations, and performance objectives to specified criterion standards.
- Conceptualize all of the interactions which occur in moving from goals to solution as a system.
- Analyze what needs to be done in solving an educational problem by performing specified tasks.
- Design how a system should function in order to accomplish its purpose, by constructing a model.
- Operate and maintain a system by performing specified tasks.
- Explain the theory of cybernetics as the key to management control.
- Explain why systems theory is necessary when interactions are complex with instantaneous effects.
- Explain the essential purpose of PERT.
- Conceptualize an instructional system as a matrix of three operations occurring on three hierarchical levels of organization.
- Prepare a planning programming budget.
- Cite the major dangers in store for the school administrator who is not prepared for the era of systems analysis.
- Explain how a systems approach can be used to promote and maintain a humanizing education.
- Perform the role of a systems manager.

John McManama

Contents

Let the Buyer Beware! 169

Avoiding the mystique of "in terms". "Cost-effectiveness".
"Accountability". "Performance objectives sold here".
The flow chart mystique. Stacking the deck. HIHO programs.
Self-fulfilling objectives. Pot-and-kettle alternatives.
Cost/benefit jazz.

The Built-In Bias for Tradition 173

Traditional objectives are easy to validate. Normative testing
rewards status quo. The better housekeeping cult.

Avoiding the Trap 176

Developing a broad base for evaluation. Analyzing the
objectives.

Humanizing the System 180

Formulating humane process goals. Developing humane
objectives and regulations. Selecting alternatives for humane
considerations. Maintaining humanized commitments
through evaluation. Creating time for humanizing.

Education in 2001 A.D. 185

A system theory of learning will be available. Instructional
units in 2001 A.D. Evaluating of behavioral change.
A unification of all sciences. Two cultures united —
2001 A.D.

Organizational goal 6.1 individualized instruction.
Administrative regulation 6.1 individualized instruction.
Program objective 6.1.1 individualized instruction.
Administrative regulation 6.1.1a individualized instruction.
Administrative regulation 6.1.1b individualized instruction.

Suggested goals for public education in Texas.

SYSTEMS ANALYSIS
FOR
EFFECTIVE
SCHOOL ADMINISTRATION

ONE

Improving School Management with a Systems Approach

This book is concerned with problem solving in the field of education. The systems approach can assist a school administrator to become a more efficient manager. Its ultimate purpose is to bring complex operations under management control.

In this first chapter we will consider the kinds of school problems for which the systems approach is most suitable. As often as possible illustrative examples will be used to demonstrate that systems theory has many direct and practical applications to educational decision making.

Chapter One will offer the school administrator the opportunity:

   ... to become familiar with the various kinds of problems for which a systems approach is suitable.
   ... to acquire a working knowledge of systems language.
   ... to analyze what needs to be done to solve a complex problem using systems analysis.
   ... to design solutions to problems using systems design.

There are many practical applications of a systems approach and it is tempting to get involved with procedures which can be put to immediate use such as PERT scheduling, PPBS budgeting, and management systems for individualized instruction, which are covered in separate chapters of this book. It is the systems approach which is the valuable tool and the major concept, and not these current applications of systems techniques.

School administrators are urged to adopt the systems approach and not the isolated management techniques which in fact are designed to accomplish only a few tasks within the total approach. Systems analysis and systems design are the tools which will be discussed in this chapter. Readers who are tempted to turn to a chapter which deals with an immediate practical concern are urged to return to this chapter before utilizing systems techniques in their schools.

"Accountability" will be a major concern of this book. Increasingly, school administrators are coming under pressure to demonstrate that they are achieving their objectives and doing so as efficiently as possible. The systems approach is directed to accountability and we will make frequent reference to techniques which are appropriate to its attainment.

"Management by objectives" is as suitable for solving educational problems as it is for problems of business management where it has been very successful. Performance objectives and appropriate management techniques will be linked throughout this book.

APPLYING A SYSTEMS APPROACH TO SCHOOL PROBLEMS

What are the kinds of decisions which confront school administrators that can be clarified by a systems approach? It is important that this is understood at the outset because many of the current school applications which are called systems approaches have been wasted on simple step-by-step problems while the kinds of complex situations which the systems approach is designed to handle are largely ignored.

If there is a goal to be accomplished where all of the tasks which are necesssary can be performed in a lineal time sequence, where there are no complex interrelationships, and where there is no need for critical management control, *it is not necessary to use a systems approach*. Good systematic step-by-step thinking will take care of this situation very nicely and the rigorous activities which are essential in systems analysis or systems design will be wasted. The school administrator who is about to schedule all of the activities which will occur in his school in the current year, including pupil activities, parent meetings, faculty meetings, and outside organizations, does not need to use a systems approach to solve his problem. These are events which will occur as discreet happenings over a period of time and any one of a number of techniques will provide a suitable schedule. Cumbersome detail should not be mistaken for complex interrelationships.

When then is a systems approach in order?

1. When complex interrelationships are involved which are difficult to manage, especially when things go wrong.
2. When otherwise simple interrelationships occur simultaneously making it difficult or impossible to correct for deviations without stopping the operation.
3. When critical feedback control must occur instantly.
4. When it is imperative to detect *all* of the social consequences of the system.
5. When it appears that the present operation could be improved by introducing any of the above elements.

What kinds of school problems meet these criteria? Actually systems analysis is appropriate for any kind of a school problem that is complex. School budgets are often simple line item affairs, but if management wished to utilize cost analysis to select the best alternative solution a systems approach is in order. Most scheduling problems are cumbersome but not complex. However, when a major organizational change is contemplated or individualized scheduling is desired, there are systems techniques which it will be worthwhile to employ. The point is that we cannot classify school problems by types because it is complexity that is the determining factor.

The federal government has served notice that it will hold school administrators accountable for the stated objectives of their programs. This means that proposals for federal funds will have to be stated in terms of measurable performance objectives. Programs will be evaluated by the degree to which objectives have been attained. One of the objectives of this book is to assist school administrators by preparing them to accept the full responsibility for accountability rather than allowing private concerns to step into this management function by default.

The chief problem to date is that we have adopted various systems techniques without putting them in the framework of a systems approach. We have gone all out to promote performance objectives, appropriate methods and means, and suitable evaluation, but we have failed to see that they have resulted in any major changes in education. The reason why our efforts to date have borne so little fruit is that we have treated each of these techniques as a total operation when in fact their value is only apparent when they are considered as a total system. We state performance objectives to describe what needs to be done. Methods and means are then selected as they are appropriate for attaining the objectives. Evaluation becomes a direct measure of the output when compared to the performance objective. It is only when the separate operations are tied together in a systems approach that the techniques prove their worth. The most important function of this book is to illustrate how this is done in connection with typical school problems.

A systems approach is basically a set of operations which is designed to help to solve problems more effectively and efficiently. It is an analytical tool without a philosophical orientation or a political bias. It cannot make value judgments or policy decisions, which remain the responsibility of the administrator, but is a powerful procedure for forcing the administrator to make his decisions systematically.

When we use a scientific technique to view our problem, we consider all of the interrelationships which are expected to occur in the process of arriving at a solution. There are several features which distinguish this approach from others:

1. All of the interrelationships which are expected to occur are combined into a single conceptual structure or system.
2. All constraints which might interfere with the solution are analyzed.
3. Alternative solutions are presented for consideration.
4. The efficiency of the system is measured in terms of cost utility.
5. A built-in information network corrects or reports any deviations of the system.

A completed systems design becomes a blueprint for action. It is not difficult to follow such a schematic outline step-by-step and arrive at the prescribed objectives. In doing this, one would function as a tactician, which is not the goal toward which this book is directed. *The administrator must function as a strategist.* He is the manager of the system and the director of the system analysts. In order to supervise the operations it is imperative that he understand system theory and administer it creatively.

This chapter is written as an introduction to the systems approach. An assumption is made that you know little about the basic principles involved, or that you would benefit from a systematic review. You may proceed directly to Chapter Two if this is not the case.

Our first order of business will be to define the terms which will be used throughout this book. Systems analysis, systems design, and systems management will be distinguished as separate operations within a systems approach. We will proceed through these three operations which must be performed in order to attain the desired end product. Finally, we will study the theory of information feedback, an effective means of regulating the system.

Developing a Systems Approach

A systems approach is a scientific method for moving from a goal to its attainment. The primary purpose of this procedure is to eliminate the discrepancy between the stated goal and the actual output. In performing the operations we are concerned with both the *effectiveness* and *efficiency* of our approach. The degree to which the actual output corresponds to our stated goal is the measure of our effectiveness. To determine our efficiency we must compare the time and energy invested with the cost utility of other methods. An efficient procedure which is ineffective makes no sense, while an effective procedure which is inefficient is wasteful.

A goal which is of considerable current interest is to individualize instruction. In the three-step systems approach we would (1) analyze what needs to be done, (2) design how to do it, and (3) manage the operation. We would insist upon a clear-cut goal statement from the governing board as an indication of their commitment, Administrative regulations and performance objectives would be written at each authority level, always responsive to the goal and increasingly specific. In the end the pupil and teacher would be informed exactly how they must perform in order to meet the goal. At the design state teaching strategies would be developed and instructional materials would be selected which would permit each individual learner to meet the criterion according to his own most efficient style. The instructional program would be managed in such a way that a constant flow of information was fed back to the pupil, the instructor, and the manager comparing progress with the goal.

This is the systems approach. The same procedure would be used for any school problem of sufficient complexity to warrant the time and effort involved. Let us assume that a school system wishes to introduce an extensive outdoor education program involving a one-week residence for all sixth graders in town. To begin with this is not a proper goal but is a *means* of attaining a goal so we would have to start by identifying the major goal to which we are responding. After the administrative regulations and performance objectives have been put in order, we would be ready to consider how to attain the goal. In a systems approach we would consider alternative methods of reaching the goal, one of which would be outdoor education. It would then be possible to compare the alternative methods using cost efficiency techniques. Once the best method was selected, a management system would be devised to monitor the operation in order to inform all concerned how well the performance matched the goal.

Several chapters of this book will be devoted exclusively to detailed systems approaches to problems in curriculum and school management so these early illustrative examples are intentionally sketchy. If the language used to this point is not clear, or the procedures are confusing, the remainder of this chapter will clarify and expand upon these ideas.

Some educators feel that a systems approach is a cold mechanical method of attacking educational problems in an era when humanistic needs are paramount. It is true that system theory has no value bias and is concerned only with achieving efficiently and effectively whatever it is that the system is designed to produce. On the other hand, if the goals and objectives of the system are directed toward humanistic ends, all of the strategies and controlling devices will be directed toward that purpose. One of the objectives of this book is to illustrate how the systems approach can be utilized to accomplish humanitarian goals.

Defining Our Terms

A systems approach has previously been cited as a scientific method for moving from a goal to its attainment. It encompasses systems analysis, systems design, and systems management. It is apparent that *systems approach* is a generic term which includes concepts which have yet to be defined: *systems analysis, systems design,* and *systems management.* It also culminates in a *system,* which is a conceptualized framework created by the systems designer. Before defining these terms we shall examine their relationship in outline form.

Problem: To get from the stated goal to the output—efficiently and effectively.

Approach: Utilize a *Systems Approach.*
1. Analyze what needs to be done. *(Systems Analysis)*
2. Design how it is to be done. *(Systems Design)*

Solution: Operate the *System.* [1]
3. Process the tasks to produce the output. *(Systems Management)*

To solve our problem with a systems approach we use systems analysis and systems design to produce a system—a set of operations for attaining the goal. The terms have been put in order and differentiated and can now be defined:

---

[1] There are times when the system is already in operation and the problem is to evaluate its efficiency. In this case analysis would be applied directly to the system which already exists.

A systems approach is a strategy which utilizes analysis, design, and management to attain a stated goal effectively and efficiently.

Systems analysis is a determination of what needs to be done in order to attain a stated goal effectively.

Systems design is a conceptual representation which makes clear how the goal is to be attained utilizing the most efficient alternative.

A system is a conceptual structure composed of interrelated functions operating as an organic unit to attain a desired output effectively and efficiently.[2]

Systems management is a procedure for monitoring the operation of a system to provide an accurate assessment of progress measured against criterion standards.

Some readers may question the omission of other relevant terminology such as cybernetics, operations research, and general systems theory. These terms and others will be defined when the discussion is specifically appropriate to the concepts which they convey.

ANALYZING WHAT NEEDS TO BE DONE

There are three operations which must be performed in a systems approach. These operations are presented in a simple flow chart model in Figure 1.

Figure 1
A Flow Chart Model of the Major Operations in a Systems Approach

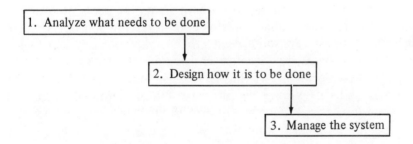

In this section we will consider the first operation: analyzing what needs to be done. Technically speaking, this first operation is systems analysis and it is better not to refer to the total systems approach as systems analysis as is often done. The term will be used consistently throughout this book to describe only the first operation of a systems approach.

---

[2] A clear-cut understanding of what a system is is an essential requirement for systems management. In Chapter Two we will consider the theory of systems in detail.

Before considering the tasks which are performed in systems analysis, we should be convinced that this method of analyzing what needs to be done is different from the way we have been operating. People have been setting goals and stating objectives throughout history. What is it that distinguishes systems analysis from the informal assessment of needs which has been going on since the caveman?

Needs assessment has always included major decisions about methods and means. The solution to a problem always introduces a new set of needs to assess. The inventors of the wheel visualized a solution but the solution itself has created unique problems for men. Needed: easy ways to make stones flat and round; ways to put holes in the center of the disk; other materials of construction in regions where there is no stone; ways to keep the wood from wearing out; ways to make the ride smoother and less bumpy; ways to keep the air from leaking out when the tire is punctured; and so on.

Process and production are an integral part of needs assessment. Solutions introduce new problems. Now it becomes easier to visualize what is happening in our modern technological era. As the solutions have become automated, instantaneous, and complex they have generated "problems of automation." We have been so happy with the solutions that we have tended to ignore the new problems. *Our ability to design solutions has exceeded our ability to analyze problems.* Systems analysis is a scientific way of analyzing complex problems and it is the best available way of contending with the problems of automation.

The major functions of systems analysis can be extracted from this presentation. We must state our major needs as goals. Our next level of needs are the terminal objectives for accomplishing the goals. In order to enable us to reach the terminal objectives we develop a solution process which in turn creates a new set of needs, the enabling objectives. A major goal of our society is to develop in our children the ability to communicate their ideas in writing. Based on our knowledge of the developmental skills of young people we establish terminal objectives which describe how the student must perform at a given time to indicate that he is making progress toward the goal. When we select linguistics as our solution method we introduce a whole new set of problems which must be analyzed as enabling objectives. These enabling objectives must be directly responsive to the terminal objectives or they are only meaningless exercises. Throughout the history of education we have treated these enabling objectives as though they were goals thus perpetuating methods that in some cases never were relevant to a major goal. Figure 2 illustrates how the functions of systems analysis are related.

Figure 2
A Flow Chart Model of the Major Functions in Systems Analysis

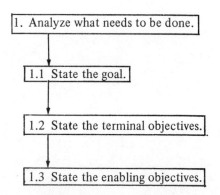

To this point we have identified three functions to be performed in systems analysis. For each function we must perform three tasks:

    A. Consider the alternatives.
    B. Establish the base criterion.
    C. Identify the constraints.

These three tasks apply to each of the three functions of systems analysis. They also apply to some of the functions of systems design and systems management as we will discover. Since these systems tasks will be recurring during all operations of the systems approach, it is convenient to think of them as the ABC procedure representing: alternatives, base criterion, and constraints.

We will be considering what is involved in performing the tasks and functions in considerable detail throughout the book. For the moment our objective is to see clearly how they are related to one another as activities to be performed. This relationship is presented in Figure 3.

Stating the Goal (1.1)

The procedure for stating the goal differs considerably from goal setting procedures of the past. Our goal statement must be explicit enough so that anyone can visualize how people or things will be different when the goal is attained. In stating the goal we are establishing the commitment of the highest authority to a given purpose. This is a very valuable statement because it will allow us to draw up administrative regulations and statements of objectives which are directed to the goal. This provides an

Figure 3
A Flow Chart Model of the ABC[3] Tasks to Be Performed in Systems Analysis

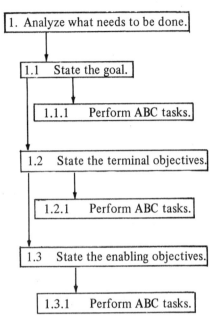

organization with a direct link between goals and performance. In analyzing what needs to be done we will be working toward two important objectives:

1. In moving from goals to objectives we will describe with increasing detail how persons or things will perform.
2. We will establish a procedure for measuring progress in comparison with the described goal.

Chapter Four is devoted entirely to illustrating how the first operation of a systems approach is conducted in connection with the practical problem of establishing goals and objectives for an elementary school mathematics program. In this chapter we will be more concerned with presenting an outline of the procedures which are involved.

Stating the goal is a policy making function. This is the specification of what needs to be done as determined by the client. The systems analyst can assist the client by outlining the procedure he must use in order to formulate his goal. Technically speaking, goal formulation is not a proper consideration for a systems approach. If clients were able to arrive at their

---

[3] ABC tasks refer to: A. Consider the alternatives, B. Establish the basic criteria, and C. Identify the constraints.

goals after carefully considering all of the decisions outlined, the analyst could begin his work with function B. Since the goal statement becomes the contract to be fulfilled, it is well worth the analyst's time to assist in translating the client's assessed needs into a well formulated goal.

The end product of function 1.1 should be a concise statement in which the goal is specified. A formulation of the goal should be brief and accurate including each of the following considerations:

1. An introductory paragraph which describes the commitment of purpose to which the goal is directed. This paragraph is usually sufficient for a complete set of goals, such as the goals of educational management.
2. A brief rationale which makes it clear *why* this goal (or these goals) are worthy of attainment.
3. A specification of the goal which provides a general indication of the performance which is sought.
4. A specification of any process goals which must be considered. These process goals are major commitments of society which indicate that the product attainment, important as it is, cannot be realized at the sacrifice of the rights of individuals. (In Chapter Four there are several examples of goal statements which include modifications in order to meet commitments to process goals.)

Care should be taken to consider goals in a much broader context than would be involved in stating objectives. The following guidelines will serve to delineate the specifications which a well-stated goal should meet:[4]

1. A goal is not concerned with explicit performance objectives.
2. The major consideration is with universals, the broad social and educational desires of society.
3. An indication of performance in broad general terms must be provided.
4. The process by which the goal will be attained should be included if a commitment to the dignity of the individual performer or learner demands a process that will not violate his integrity.

Appendix A illustrates the practical value of good goal statements. In this Connecticut town the board of education has indicated its commitment to individualized instruction. The school administrators were then able to write administrative regulations and performance objectives which make explicit how the schools must organize and how teachers and students must perform in order to demonstrate that they are working

---

[4] Examples of goals written to these specifications are presented for school mathematics in Chapter Four, for individualized instruction in Appendix A, and for a complete set of educational goals in Appendix B.

toward the goal of individualized instruction. It should be apparent that a school system which had a complete set of regulations and objectives for each major goal, drawn up as specifically as those in Appendix A, would have taken a giant step toward accountability. Certainly there would be a clear idea about what everyone was expected to do to attain the goal extending right down the line from the board of education and superintendent to the teacher and student.

The implication to this point is that we know what our goal is and only need to state it in accepted form. In actual practice the most critical problem facing educators is uncertainty concerning what the goals are. For the remainder of this section we will review the specific tasks to be performed in formulating the goal (the ABC tasks).

Consider the alternatives. (1.1.1a) What is the status of things here and now, before any tasks have been undertaken? This condition is so obvious that it is often neglected, but it must not be overlooked. What is apparent to the client may be obscure to the systems analyst. The more the analyst knows about the present operation, the better will be the service which he can offer. Any descriptive materials which are available to provide answers to the following questions will prove useful:

1. What is the goal of *present* operations?
2. What functions are being performed?
3. What methods are used to attain these functions?
4. *Why is a change necessary?*

Whenever expressed needs are formulated as goals, there is an implicit hypothesis that the goal is the best possible solution to the problem. If those who operate within the system accept the goal as a directive, those who formulate the goal must be certain that they have postulated the best interpretation of what needs to be done since in many cases there are other goals which might satisfy the same need. The following checklist will serve as a route of investigation for other alternatives:

1. Has the client's indication of a desired change been interpreted correctly?
2. Is the client open to consideration of a revision of the goal?
3. Is the goal statement broad enough to allow for flexibility in establishing objectives? (Goals which indicate in any way *how* the goal is to be reached preempt the rights of those whose responsibility is to determine the methods and means of attaining the goal.)
4. Is the goal completely responsive to the desires of those who will be affected?
5. Is the effort and energy applied to the system well spent or should other more important or relevant goals be considered?

Establish the base criterion measure. (1.1.1b) Our task here is to focus on the thing which is to be processed by the system. This could be a child in an instructional system, financial accounts in a program budget, or a vessel in a ship building operation. This thing to be processed will be called the *purposive input* to differentiate it from other inputs which will be described later. The term purposive is used here to denote an input which it is the purpose of the system to produce or process.

Why is it necessary to describe the purposive input? *We must describe the input accurately because the difference between the input and the output will become one of the measures of the effectiveness of our system.* Each characteristic of the input which is destined to be changed must be quantitatively described if possible so that we can later determine how much change has taken place. This measurement must be applied before the system is implemented because once the processing begins, the opportunity to describe the original input status will be lost forever.

If our goal in an instructional system were to increase the critical thinking ability of the student, it is obvious that we must start with an assessment of his present ability to think critically. What is less obvious is that the test which has been selected must provide an accurate assessment of *both the present status and the end product status.* Many gains which occur in modern math programs will not be detected by most stand-ardized achievement tests. If an adequate test is found at the conclusion of the course to properly evaluate the results it will then be too late to obtain a comparable input score.

The status of input measures is most important when dealing with instructional systems. Implied in all instructional objectives is the preface, "To take the student from where he is to . . ." It becomes obvious that when we talk about effectiveness our statistics will not be impressive unless we can also indicate the amount of change which has occurred.

The statement of the desired change provides the data for the performance measure. We should not be concerned about going beyond this statement because we will be writing performance objectives for each operation before we are finished. It will be necessary to consider how to measure the standards and specifications which have been prescribed for the end product. Whereas the statement of the desired change identifies what is to be done, the performance measure indicates *how we can be certain that we have reached our goal.* In order to do this we must indicate the kind of behavior or performance which can be expected as evidence that the goal has been reached and the standard of performance which will be considered acceptable.

There are several important points to be considered when establishing output standards for goal attainments:

1. The output statement is a description of ends, not methods and means. We are interested at this point in a general description of the ultimate behavior required for acceptable performance. Any description which specifies the means to be used must be justified as a desire of society. To be able to express one's self effectively in writing is an appropriate instructional goal. To be able to diagram a sentence is unacceptable as a goal since it describes the means to an end. The criterion for acceptable performance should be based on goal attainment and not on techniques of instruction.[5]

2. *Output measures need not be specific since they are supported by performance objectives.* There is no need to describe performance in any detail since we will be establishing performance objectives for each operation, function, and task. These will be considered in detail in section 1.2. It is advisable to be familiar with the purpose of performance objectives before writing output measures since this will prevent needless repetition.

3. *Output measures are not restricted to utilitarian or cognitive goals.* The major sin which is committed in establishing output measures is restricting consideration to behavior which can be measured easily. Most of the goals which are cited for fine arts education are not utilitarian but their importance is not diminished because of this. Goals which deal with attitudes and appreciations are often as important as those which are concerned with cognition, although they are more difficult to assess. Our concern is to describe behavior which is desirable before we attempt to measure it. Those who consider only that which is measurable to be desirable eliminate many worthwhile goals in the process.

It should now be evident why the goal statement must give some indication of performance. These output standards become the gauge for measuring the degree of goal attainment.

It should also be apparent why we describe our goal as a product. The product measure establishes at a given time whether or not the system is producing the product desired. Since we are in the systems analysis operation our concern is with the product and we must deal with measures of effectiveness. We can also measure the efficiency of the process, but this determination is considered as a systems design problem.

In establishing our performance measure we are identifying the indicators which will be accepted as the criterion for successful performance. In the case of manufactured products we can establish detailed specifications and require that the output is an exact replica of the goal statement. Evaluation is then a straightforward measurement process. When we are dealing with social systems and human behavior we are

---

[5] An important exception to this rule is "process goals" which do in fact deal with methods of instruction. Process goals will be considered in Chapter Three as a special case in formulating goals.

confronted with a far more complex procedure. We must then identify indicators which will be accepted as evidence that the output state has been achieved. Almost all instructional measurement falls into this category.

There is a final aspect of acquiring product measures which represents the real contribution of systems thinking to the evaluation process. A system should automatically provide feedback information about the product being processed. As soon as the product varies critically from the desired state, the system should either report this information, correct the condition automatically, screen out the malformation, or stop. A good screw machine performs all of these functions in one continuous operation. When we deal with social systems we must invent ways to provide this same kind of feedback information. End of year examinations exemplify the poorest form of feedback. It is information which arrives too late to inform the student or affect the present instruction. End of unit mastery tests would be somewhat more useful. The ideal type of information is that which is fed back from a computer to report instantly for each student as many factors as are available as frequently as is desired.

Most of the chapters which follow contain precise statements of the input and output measures related to the goals sought. Further clarification is presented in Chapters Three and Four where goals and objectives are examined in detail and the proper technique for writing goals which contain sufficient specification for performance measurement are developed and illustrated.

Identify the constraints. (1.1.1c) What factors have made it difficult to achieve the present goal? It may well be that these same constraints will need to be considered in the system to be designed. If certain constraints made a change necessary it is imperative that they be identified.

The most common error made by analysts when performing this task is one of overlooking areas in which goal interference can occur. The analyst should prepare a checklist which will force the administrator to make a complete input to output examination. Questions such as the following should be considered:

1. Are the input resources adequate? (Consider all the resources needed to do the job; finances, material, and personnel.)
2. What contingencies are interfering with progress? (Contingencies are influences which are not a planned part of the operations but which could affect the functioning of the system. Natural catastrophes, mechanical breakdown, and psychological resistance should be considered.)

3. Are the tasks relevant to the goal? (Tasks which are performed very efficiently might nevertheless have little effect on goal attainment. If so they are constraints to effectiveness.)
4. Are efficient methods being used? (There are times when the end product conforms exactly to output standards but the cost in time or resources is out of line. Outdated methods are one such constraint to efficiency.)
5. Is the system being adequately monitored? (There must be provisions for frequent and reliable evaluation concerning how well the system is meeting its objectives. Inadequate monitoring is a constraint to management control.)

Note that we are concerned with constraints to present operations and not the new system. An analysis of interference and resistence in current operation will provide valuable data for the design of the new system.

Stating the Terminal Objectives (1.2)

There has probably been more written concerning objectives than any other aspect of systems analysis. The terms "performance objectives," "behavioral outcomes," "instructional objectives," and "management objectives" are all in common usage. In our view they all refer to the same function, so whenever we refer broadly to objectives in this book we will use the term "performance objectives." There is an important difference between end objectives which are related directly to the goal and means objectives which refer to the methods and means of producing the goal. To indicate this distinction we will refer to terminal objectives and enabling objectives as types of performance objectives whenever the distinction is necessary. Otherwise the term "performance objectives" will describe both functions.

Consider alternative objectives. (1.2.1a) The identification of alternative solutions is an important characteristic of a systems approach. The administrator who operates true to prescribed form will insist that he is presented with alternative solutions so that he can take part in the choice of the best available solution. In this task both efficiency and effectiveness are taken into consideration. That solution which offers the best combination of both will be selected. There are certain key questions to be answered in searching out alternative procedures:

1. How effective is the solution in terms of achieving the goal? (Index of goal attainment.)
2. How effective is the solution in terms of producing a change? (Index of change.)

3. Are new and better resources available?
4. Is the procedure feasible in terms of cost efficiency?
5. Are there humane factors which would make alternative procedures more desirable even though somewhat less productive?

Establish the base criterion measure for each objective. (1.2.1b) When systems engineers apply their skills in industry they take the goal and list the specifications which the product must have in order to meet goal standards. These specifications are precise and explicit and describe what the final product must look like and how it must function. These specifications become the objectives of the system. Performance objectives in industrial applications do the following:

1. Describe in detail what the finished product must look like and how it will function. (Nomenclature)
2. Specify the conditions under which it will function as stated. (Specifications)
3. Specify the standard of performance which will be acceptable. (Standards)

Systems thinking had to be applied to instructional systems with the advent of programmed learning. Programmers found that the objectives available in courses of study and textbooks were as general as the goal itself. In order to write learning programs it became necessary to write the objectives in the kind of language that systems engineers would use.

It would be difficult to improve upon the work of Mager[6] when specifying the tasks performed in preparing instructional objectives.

> "*First,* identify the terminal behavior by name; you can specity the kind of behavior that will be accepted as evidence that the learner has achieved the objective.
> *Second,* try to define the desired behavior further by describing the important conditions under which it will occur.
> *Third,* specify the criteria of acceptable performance by describing how well the learner must perform to be considered acceptable."

An example of an instructional objective written to these specifications will contain the three requirements in one statement:[7]

At the completion of the sixth reader the student will demonstrate

---

[6] Robert Mager, *Preparing Instructional Objectives.* (Palo Alto, Calif.: Fearon Publishers, Inc., 1962) p. 12.

[7] Numerous performance objectives are presented for elementary school mathematics in Chapter Four.

mastery by reading orally a short selection from a sixth reader within four minutes, making not more than four recognition errors in 100 words.

Many writers have expressed their disappointment in the fact that Mager's performance objectives are not more extensively used in schools. His book has become a classic reference and few authors have attempted to improve upon his efforts. The problem would seem to be not that Mager's objectives are inadequate but that practitioners are unable to relate them to their needs. There are two additional factors which must be present before curriculum designers and instructors can utilize performance objectives as they were intended:

1. The educational practitioner must perceive the relationship between objectives, teaching strategy, and evaluation. In other words the concept of an instructional system must be fully comprehended before performance objectives can be used effectively. (In Chapter Three a complete instructional system will be analyzed.)
2. Performance objectives tell what is to be done but not *why*. A rationale should be written to justify for the learner and the instructor why a particular performance is worth accomplishing.

Neither the stated goal nor the objectives will indicate why the desired output is worth attaining. When the systems approach was first adopted for use in social systems the impersonal procedures of mechanical and electrical systems were retained. It soon became apparent that the system needed to be humanized in order to operate successfully where people were involved.

Canfield[8] can be credited with developing a tool which makes objectives meaningful. He was concerned with instructional systems and recommended a statement of rationale which would indicate to the learner and the instructor why each objective should be achieved. It would seem that in any system where people are affected by the operations, a rationale would make the system more acceptable.

Identify the constraints to performance. (1.2.1c) A constraint is any factor which is likely to interfere with the attainment of the objective. Any of the input factors could be considered to be constraints, especially when the system calls for them to be increased. All school administrators will appreciate this in relation to a need for additional financial resources.

---

8 Albert Canfield, "A Rationale for Performance Objectives." *Audio Visual Instruction,* February, 1968, pp. 127-129.

Even though constraints are unique to each system it is possible to identify where to look for them.

1. *Input constraints.* Inputs to a system can be classified as either purposives or facilities. Purposive inputs are the things we are trying to change while facilities are the resources available to bring about the change. In an instructional system the student is a purposive input. Schools, teachers, and books are facility inputs. We can now direct our attention to potential constraints in the input by considering each in turn.

   In social systems each purposive input is a unique organism. If the system is not flexible enough to accept the variety of characteristics among individual inputs, the uniqueness of input itself could be considered to be a constraint. *Each purposive input with characteristics or needs not anticipated by the system is a constraint.*

   The facility inputs to the system also vary in kind and degree. *Each facility input which does not perform as expected is a constraint.*

   There is also an assumption that the facilities will be available at the time and in the quantity desired. *Facility inputs which arrive "too little or too late" must also be considered as constraints.*

2. *Contingencies.* Anything which might happen along the way from input to output which will influence the change taking place in a manner not planned is a contingency. Each operation must be examined for its own constraints. Contingencies can be fortuitous but we are concerned with those undesirable events that interfere with progress. Since this is a scientific procedure we are only interested in those contingencies which affect the desired output and in effect become inputs to the system.

   The single best source of possible constraints is past experience. We look for operations which are as similar as possible to our project and investigate the kinds of constraints which were encountered. A small eastern town about to consider a new course in sex education would do well to find out what has happened in other small towns where this program was started.

It is difficult to generalize about constraints. As we discuss program budgets, instructional systems, and other systems approaches, the constraints which are unique to these procedures will be identified. Beyond this all that can be offered are three questions to consider:

1. What contraints have arisen in projects which are similar?
2. Who will be affected by the changes proposed?
3. What procedures might cause adverse psychological reaction?

Stating the Enabling Objectives (1.3)

We are now confronted with our first indication that the systems approach is not a simple step-by-step procedure. At this point we are about to consider the objectives which relate to the solution method and we have not yet discussed the solution, which is the concern of the second operation, design the system. Obviously we will have to wait until the method has been selected before we can consider the enabling objectives.

Fortunately the procedures for deriving the enabling objectives are identical to those used in establishing the terminal objectives. When the design operation is completed refer to 1.2, 1.2.1a, 1.2.1b, and 1.2.1c which are equally appropriate for writing enabling objectives.

The distinction between terminal objectives and enabling objectives will be made clearer in Chapter Three and Chapter Four when we deal with the hierarchy of objectives in reference to an instructional system.

DESIGNING THE SYSTEM

Everything which has been done to this point has been a preparation for the moment at hand; design the system. This is the second operation of the model of a systems approach presented in Figure 1, designing how it is to be done. It is also the operation commonly referred to as systems design.

There are four functions to be performed in designing the system. Figure 4 illustrates how the functions of systems design are related.

Figure 4
A Flow Chart Model of the Major Functions in Systems Design

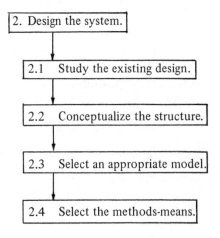

Obviously the design of individual systems will vary greatly from others so that it is impossible to blueprint a master design as a solution to all problems. What will be provided is a set of functions and tasks which apply to all systems. We will consider a model of a total system which indicates the relationship among goals, analysis and design. This same model will also indicate the flow from input to process to output and will outline the management control network.

Study the Existing Design (2.1)

Many times when a systems designer begins his task there is a process already in operation which needs to be changed. In those cases where the designer will operate in virgin territory, function 2.1 will be unnecessary.

It is important to know why a change is desired. If a system has been operating for a period of time there is available a great deal of information which is pertinent to the new design. The fact that the old system is outmoded because of ineffectiveness or inefficiency does not rule out a study of this operation for valuable data. Constraints which were observed in the old system may remain as factors to be considered in the new system. It would be folly to ignore this rich source of experience and data.

Perhaps the most important investigation to be undertaken is to determine whether or not the goals and objectives have changed. Often dissatisfaction with a present operation is laid to inefficiency when the real problem is that the objectives were changed without anyone realizing that this has occurred. If this is the case, the new system will soon run into the same problem. If the objectives must be changed the whole operation will be thrown back into the hands of the systems analyst, but there would be no point in proceeding in any other way.

Conceptualize the Structure (2.2)

System and structure are related concepts. When we create a system we conceptualize a structure. In the science of rocketry, structuring is the straightforward problem of providing a form for a function. The lunar space vehicle LEM is a case in point. LEM had to be large enough to perform its functions and small enough to be carried in the mother rocket. Flight patterns dictated one form, maneuverability another, and landing a third. Little by little, function determined form and constraints modified form until a final structure appeared. This conceptualized structure was the model which became the prototype for future vehicles.

Unless there is a structure there is no system. Many of the procedures which are called systems approaches do not culminate in a designed system. A plan for scheduling resources so that they will arrive where they are needed when they are needed is known as linear programming. This is a logistical flowchart procedure which is often used in connection with system design. Taken by itself it does not qualify as a system because it has no structure. Considered alone, none of the tasks described in this chapter can be called a systems approach. *The systems approach is the sum total of tasks leading to the formulation of an operating structure.* School administrators should treat skeptically any proposals which purport to be systems approaches on the justification that they involve some systems tasks as procedures.[9]

Figure 5
A Structural Concept of the Components of a Systems Design

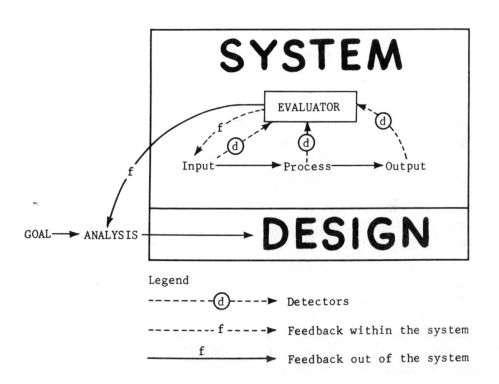

---

[9] This warning is expanded in Chapter Eight where pitfalls of the systems approach are discussed.

The conceptualized structure contains the major elements of a systems approach. This task requires that we proceed through all of these elements and conceptualize how our systems network will function. There are several of these networks which have not yet been discussed, such as the input-process—output-network and the detector-evaluator loops. It is necessary to present our systems model (Figure 5) at this point since it is relevant to this task. All of the information needed to understand how this model operates will be presented in this chapter.

Select an Appropriate Model (2.3)

When we design a system, we construct a model which stands for the real life system proposed. A model of a fuel system is as much a system in all respects as is the fuel system in an automobile.

Models may be physical devices, flow charts, mathematical equations, or descriptive statements. If you were to survey the literature you would find that most writers resort to flow charts to conceptualize their systems. Leonard Silvern conducted such a survey over a period of many years, and the results are published in his *Systems Engineering of Education I.*[10] Of the more than eighty figures presented in this publication, all but eight are flow charts. (The exceptions are four graphic analogs, two circuit diagrams, one Venn diagram, and one dynamic forecasting conceptualization, the last of which was nothing more than a pictorial flow chart.) Although mathematical models were discussed, none were developed to the model level.

A good many of the flow charts which are encountered in current literature are not models of systems at all and, in truth, represent the linear type of thinking which we wish to supersede. Extreme forms may be seen in which each word in a phrase is placed in a separate box with interconnecting arrows. It is unfortunate that a "flow chart mystique" is the greatest barrier to communication in systems theory when in fact the function of the model is to clarify and make comprehensible.

The mathematical equation is the ultimate format for models since it provides a high degree of sensitivity for management control. Mathematical equations are more difficult to apply to social systems but do have some present applications.

---

[10] Leonard Silvern, *Systems Engineering of Education I: The Evolution of Systems Thinking in Education,* (Los Angeles, Calif.: Education and Training Consultants Co., 1965).

Select the Methods-Means (2.4)

With a conceptualized structure and a model on hand we are ready to select the methods and means of implementing the design. Now we must select the components, materials, and personnel which can best accomplish each objective.

When we know not only what is to be accomplished (goal) but also how it is to be accomplished (objective) we can select the components and operating specifications for each objective. It should be apparent that if we had started designing the system by selecting the components we would have a series of fragmented tasks which, although sequential, would not be aware of their totality. We considered the structure of the system and developed a model in order to avoid this narrow view.

The selection of the components is both a science and an art. In Chapter Five, we will select the components for instructional systems and indicate some of the factors which need to be considered in determining the suitability of materials for designated tasks. The following checklist is provided as a guide to decision-making in the process of selecting input-process—output-components:

1. Compile a list of all components which are suitable to perform each function.
2. List all performance specifications for each component.
3. List all design limits prescribed by the client or determined by the analyst.
4. Determine the effectiveness of the component.
5. Determine the efficiency of the component.
6. Match the components to the individual characteristics of the purposive input.

Identify alternative components. (2.4a) The investigation of resources will suggest alternative solutions. Newer automated equipment could increase efficiency. The available staff might be reduced by improving scheduling and deployment. A large initial cost of automating might be offset by lower operating cost. Each procedure should be outlined sufficiently so that a cost analysis is possible.

The key factor in selecting from available alternatives will be the comparative indices of effectiveness and efficiency. The investigation of possible alternatives should contain all data that is needed in order to make accurate measurements of productivity. If there are constraints that will offset advantages they should be noted.

In Defense Department procedures, the preparation of alternatives is a major operation. Each alternative is researched as carefully as all others in order to prevent bias. A prejudiced presentation would not survive the rigorous investigation which each proposal would receive. Even though school administrators do not have the staff needed to emulate this procedure they should be impressed by the tremendous importance that is assigned to task 2.4a by the Federal Government.

SUMMARY

In identifying the kinds of school problems for which a systems approach is suitable, emphasis was directed to problems in which there were complex interrelationships which are difficult to manage, such as, cost-analysis of alternative solutions to the goal of a project, pupil scheduling in instances where a major organizational change is contemplated, and management control of an individualized program of instruction.

The meaning of such systems terms as systems analysis, systems design, systems management, system, goal, performance objectives, terminal objectives, and enabling objectives were clarified.

The functions of systems analysis were identified and described as, (1) state the goal, (2) state the terminal objectives, and (3) state the enabling objectives.

The functions of systems design were identified and described as, (1) study the existing design, (2) conceptualize the structure, (3) select an appropriate model, and (4) select the method-means.

The third operation of a systems approach, manage the system, has not yet been considered. Systems management will be analyzed in Chapter Two. We will also examine the theory of systems because this is where the real power of the approach lies and the manager of the system is the person who must understand the theory of management control. As often as possible practical techniques such as PERT scheduling will be presented along with the theory as a reminder that we are dealing with a tool which has a high payoff in utilitarian value.

TWO

Managing the System

The successful manager of a complex organization which utilizes a systems approach must have a working knowledge of systems theory. The major breakthrough which systems theory has brought to management is a high-leverage method of controlling what is happening in the system. This is the most valuable chapter in this book because it presents the key ideas which make the systems approach so powerful. This chapter is designed to enable the school administrator:

... to apply management control to a system by organizing a network of detectors and evaluators which provide information about what is happening in the system.
... to explain why automation has forced us to devise new methods of managing organizations.
... to explain what a system is and why it works.
... to gain some appreciation of cybernetics as a high-leverage method of controlling a system.
... to learn how to use a work breakdown schedule (WBS) and a program evaluation review technique (PERT) for scheduling the sequence of complex tasks.

APPLYING MANAGEMENT CONTROL

In Chapter One we examined the tasks which have to be performed in systems analysis and systems design. The third and final operation to be performed in a systems approach is applying management control, also referred to as systems management. This is the operation which should be of greatest interest to school administrators. In many cases there will be other personnel in the school system who perform the functions of systems design and systems analysis. Systems management hits home. This is the operation which provides management control of the system and no informed school administrator would want to be unaware of how his system was being controlled. In cases where programs have built-in control systems, we want to be certain that this information comes directly to the administrator who has line authority over the program. In other instances where programs do not have provisions for feeding progress information to the line administrator, we will want to build in the necessary detectors and evaluators to provide this data. This first section will outline the procedures which will place the school administrator in a position where all of the feedback arrows lead straight to his office.

The flowchart model for the third operation is rather simple but together with the models previously presented it completes the systems approach.

Figure 6
A Flow Chart Model of the Third and Final Operation—Applying the Management Control

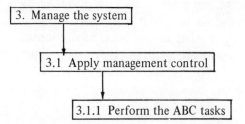

We apply management control by inserting detectors into the system at critical points which feed back information about how the system is functioning compared to criterion standards. If we want to know how a student is progressing relative to performance objectives, our detectors will be criterion tests. These measurements of mastery are different from the usual achievement tests because they are directed specifically to the objectives and measure the degree to which they have been achieved. In all cases, the detectors are devices for monitoring performance specified by performance objectives. If we wish to know how our long range building program is progressing, the detectors would be regular reports of progress from supervisors which permit the administrator to compare actual construction to the schedule of construction established by the PERT. (This planning, evaluating, and reviewing technique will be described later in this chapter.)

It should be clear from Figures 5, 7, and 9 that detectors can be inserted at any point of the operation where the administrator feels that a progress report is critical. This has been done at the input state in Figure 7 and at the output state in Figure 8.

The detector reports only what is happening without judging whether the results are satisfactory. We must feed information from the detector to an evaluator in order to provide this judgment. There are two methods of monitoring progress—automatic monitoring and feedback reports. The criterion test cited above is an example of automatic monitoring. Each test will have a criterion standard. If, in the example given, the standard was 85% correct, the test itself would determine whether mastery had been attained. The student who scores less than 85% will be directed to further activities in the same unit while one who scores 90% will move automatically to the next unit. The supervisor's report of progress on construction is an example of the second type of evaluation. In this case the administrator is the evaluator and he will make the judgment concerning the acceptability of progress.

In Figures 5, 7, and 8 there are separate loops to evaluators from the detectors. Again they can occur at any stage of the operation. The evaluators in turn feed back corrections to the system automatically as illustrated in Figures 5 and 7 by the dotted arrow back to the input, or in reports as indicated by the solid arrow fed back to the analysis operation.

Since the nature of the input, process, and output differ, we will examine each of them to discover the management control process at work.

Figure 7
A Schematic Representation of the Feedback Loop at Work in the Input Stage

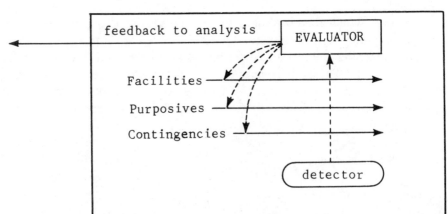

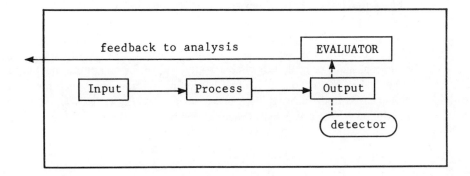

Figure 8
A Schematic Representation of the Feedback Loop at Work in the Output Stage

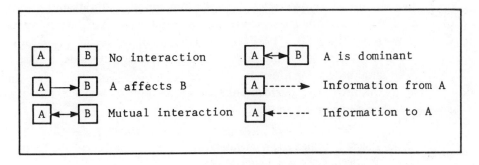

Figure 9
A Coding of the Interrelationships Which Occur Within a System

1. *Input control.* We have seen how the input consists of facilities, purposives, and contingencies. Feedback input can now be added to this list. Detectors in the input stage report quantitative information about each of the three input stages to the evaluator. As can be seen in Figure 5, the evaluator can feed automatic correction to the individual stages or report the condition to the analyst as indicated by the solid feedback arrow. It is the systems designer's task to select the appropriate detectors and evaluators and place them wherever they are needed in the system.

2. *Process control.* The process is the set of interrelationships which convert the input to the output. We must be concerned with all relevant interaction including that of parts to the whole. The feedback loops work in the same manner here but are a little more complex because of the interrelationships among

various functions. Figure 9 presents a coding system for the flowcharts used in this book and indicates the nature of important interactions in the processing stage including feedback.

3. *Output control.* The output is the actual product to be compared to the desired product or goal. The system is effective to the extent that the output is equivalent to the goal. It is often important to know how much the input was changed in the process, especially in instructional systems. No matter how poorly the system was designed there is usually a detector at this stage.

Measure Against the Base Criterion (3.1.1b)

Most systems approaches designate evaluation as a separate function. This has not been done in this book because of the firm belief that *evaluation occurs during all functions and must be planned before the operations begin.* In the first operation, systems analysis, we established the criterion base for the goal and specified it further in the terminal objectives. At the systems design stage we developed methods and means of production and from these came the enabling objectives which again were relevant to the goal. The evaluation network connects all of these tasks and insures that the evaluators of systems management are accountable to the same base criterion.

When we monitor the performance of the system as managers we are asking two basic questions:

1. How efficiently is the system operating?
2. How effectively is the system operating?

Measurements of efficiency deal with expenditures of energy, usually in terms of time or money. How does the elapsed time compare with the schedule or the PERT? How does the present cumulative cost compare with the cost projection?

Measurements of effectiveness refer to performance. How does the present progress compare to the expected progress? Ultimately the end product must be measured in comparison to the stated goal.

Identify the Constraints to Management Control (3.1.1c)

The constraints to management control refer to anything which might interfere with good information feedback, accurate evaluation, or effective correction of deviations of the system. The validity and reliability of the detectors and evaluators are of crucial concern here. Validity is the extent to which we are monitoring performance directed to the stated criterion. Reliability is the degree to which our monitoring devices are consistent in their accuracy of reporting. When we select achievement tests which are only vaguely connected to stated performance objectives, we are guilty of using detection procedures which are not valid. When our evaluation instruments do not provide the same information under identical circumstances they are unreliable. One of the gravest errors encountered in school applications of a systems approach is that our detectors and evaluators are not valid and reliable indicators of stated performance objectives. This pitfall is serious and will be dealt with in greater detail in Chapter Eight.

AUTOMATION:
The New Technology

Automation may seem to be a rather remote concern for school administrators faced with the stress of daily problems. On the contrary, it is only when automation is involved that a systems approach is worth pursuing. We are not referring to automated devices such as thermostats, or even the more complex computer. The automated process which concerns us here are complete automated systems: individualized instructional programs with built-in tests and prescriptions which are available to the learner automatically, learning disabilities programs which classify students and route them through prescribed activities, or management control of a school transportation system in a large city. The tools and techniques of automation are at hand but we are still thinking in mechanical step-by-step procedures. Mechanization can be managed by observation. *Automation can only be managed by conceptualizing it as a behaving system and then making the behavior responsive to planning.*

In order to appreciate why systems thinking is such an urgent need, it is necessary to understand how automation differs from mechanization. In mechanical processes things occur sequentialy across a span of time. These systems can be made larger or can be made to work faster, but whatever change takes place always occurs in sequence. When we work with or create mechanical systems we can think in terms of cause and effect working in sequence across a time span. This poses no special problems because man is well equipped mentally to think abstractly about things which have concrete counterparts. The fact that a time span is involved makes it possible to break up the operation into fragments which can be dealt with one at a time. This is systematic sequential thinking and it is perfectly suitable for dealing with mechanical problems. Automation is another matter!

Automation may include mechanical procedures, but in concept and process it is much more than efficient mechanization. We are no longer dealing with time spans because things now happen simultaneously rather than sequentially. Processes which can be united instantaneously as one function possess an organic unity which becomes more important than the sum of the parts involved. In order to think about or create automated processes, we must deal with the total effect at any given moment or we will be left standing at the starting gate.

Marshall McCluhan dealt with this phenomenon in a brilliant insightful manner in *Understanding Media: The Extensions of Man.*

> Automation is not an extension of the mechanical principles of fragmentation and separation of operations. It is rather the invasion of the mechanical world by the instantaneous character of electricity. That is why those involved in automation insist that it is a way of thinking, as much as it is a way of doing. Instant synchronization of numerous operations has ended the old mechanical pattern of setting up operations in a linear sequence. The assembly line has gone the way of the stag line.[1]

Instantaneous processing is one of two unique characteristics of automation, instant corrective feedback is the other. Some portion of the energy is diverted to correct deviations from systems specifications. We now have added a new dimension to our operation in that we can feed information back to an earlier function *instantaneously.*

We will be examining cybernetics, the theory behind automation, in this chapter so nothing more needs to be said about feedback at this time. If the actual operations themselves still have a phantom quality about them, the clue to the mystery is in McCluhan's reference to the character of electricity. It was electricity that gave automation its most unique characteristic and it is electrical circuitry which makes synchronization and instant feedback possible.

If automation is already here and working well, why are we so concerned about finding ways to think about it? There are a number of good reasons:

1. Small automated systems, no matter how well they work, are poor testimony

---

[1] Marshall McCluhan, *Understanding Media: The Extensions of Man,* (New York: McGraw Hill Book Company, 1963) p. 349.

to the potential of automation. The breakthrough to large complex systems can only come about with systems thinking.

2. Mechanical units tend toward one task specialization; automated units have the potential to perform many tasks in one specialized function. (This insight comes again from McCluhan who cited the tailpipe fabricating unit which has the capability of turning out as many as eighty different styles in any sequence in one continuous operation with no more difficulty than if it were programmed to produce only one model.)

3. We humans have a tendency to persist in doing what we can do well rather than what we should do. (Witness the highly sophisticated manner in which we solve our problems of space exploration in comparison to our failure to solve the relatively simple problem of substandard housing.)

4. Mechanization causes a series of discrete effects which are visible and manageable. Automation results in a composite behavior with many effects. (We cannot afford to stand by myopically waiting for our specific desired effects while unnoticed by-products bury us.)

Once again we have found that systems thinking and cybernetics are the keys to managing and operating systems. With this background we will take another look at systems theory as a technique for thinking about performance in the framework of organization.

SYSTEM THEORY:
A New Way of Looking at Organizations

A system is a conceptual structure composed of interrelated functions operating to attain a desired output effectively and efficiently. Note that a system is a *conceptual* structure, that it is invented as a device for understanding interrelated activities. Systems do not exist in nature; only organisms and objects exist. Systems are the way we perceive things as interrelated functions in order to work with them or talk about them. The circulatory system in the human body is not a complete closed system. Among other things it depends upon the liver, which is part of the digestive system, for glucose. Neither of these systems exist as completely independent self-sustaining entities. Systems were *invented by men as a way of perceiving relationships.*

When things interact with each other, we create a mental model to explain the whole process. Although many of the parts of the system may be visible as "real things" the whole system is an intellectual construct which is available to the senses only through models. The word "synergistic" was coined to convey the idea that a whole is something more then the sum of its parts. This "something more" consists of the interrelationships, functions, and processes which are relevant to a specific outcome.

Each system which we can describe is a subsystem of some other system. In turn, each system usually has several subsystems. Some parts of a
system may also be parts of bigger systems and all open systems interact
with others. When looked at from below, a set of organisms or objects
may be perceived as a system and yet, without destroying this concept,
the same set of interactions viewed from above are only operations or
functions of a larger system. This Janus-like quality of the hierarchy of
organization is clearly described by Arthur Koestler[2] who invented the
word "holon" to describe this phenomenon. This brilliant conceptualization has far greater implications than can be conveyed here and the reference should be read by any serious student of system theory.

When we discover how complex interactions can be we should appreciate why we find it easier to isolate specific functions and think of them
as a system in order to better understand what is happening. A school
system is a subsystem of our educational system. Within a school system
we have an instructional system, an administrative system, a curriculum
system, and an interpersonal system. The instructional system is, in part,
composed of the reading system which contains the phonics system—and
so forth. A globe in a classroom would have to be considered in the
instructional system and in the administrative system. Again we can see
why it is desirable to have well designed systems to aid our comprehension.

When we create a system from a large complex operation we work
down to the largest set of interrelationships which are relevant to the
outcome which interests us. When we construct a system beginning with
simple phenomena, we build up to the largest set of interrelationships
which we can comprehend. Any system must have been comprehensible
to someone at some time by definition. When we find a system to be too
complex to be manageable, we invent subsystems which are not fragmented units but complete systems in themselves.

The System Itself — Why It Works

A system is a network of parts interacting as an organic unit to perform
a function. When we think in terms of systems our objective is to make
these networks responsive to human management. Where systems exist in
nature we analyze them to discover how they are organized in order to
increase our knowledge about the world. When we create systems we do
so in order to take advantage of the superior effectiveness and efficiency

---

[2] Arthur Koestler, *The Ghost in the Machine,* (New York: The Macmillan Company,
1967).

which result when all of the energy which is generated is under management control.

We look to a system for solutions when we are confronted with a problem which is too complex to respond to lineal analysis. When the interrelationships are complex, when the expertise of several disciplines must be combined toward the solution of a problem, when functions occur simultaneously, or when feedback correction is essential, a systems approach will most likely provide the best solution and the effort expended in analyzing and designing a systems will be well spent.

In order to fully appreciate what a system is and what it can do, it is necessary to understand the concept of *organic unity*. Whenever a group of parts work together to produce an effect in an instant of time we have a situation which is different from a cause and effect sequence in several vital ways. When a group of parts work in mechanical sequence, we have a situation where A causes B in a certain amount of time. When this action is completed, B causes C in the next time sequence, and so forth, as illustrated in Figure 10.

Figure 10
Performance Sequence in a Mechanical Cause and Effect Sequence

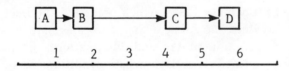

This series of events is lineal and mechanical and can be controlled by observation. Now let us see what happens when events are automated.

If we were to start at D and push the chain of events so that they were compressed back to zero, we would not have a speeded up process, but an instant process. *The chain of events would cease to exist and organic unity would be the result.* It is necessary to comprehend this phenomenon in order to appreciate the nature of a system because we can no longer rely on mechanical cause and effect thinking to solve problems where instantaneous actions and reactions are occurring. We cannot think in terms of summation where there is organic unity. The total effect of parts working together is always something more than the sum of the parts. In order to understand what is happening in a system, or to gain management control, we must devise a conceptual model of what is happening and utilize the high-leverage power of cybernetics to control production in order to meet performance objectives.

System Theory in Military Operations

Military strategists are far ahead of the field in the area of the application of system theory to problems and decisions. Military problems are conceived of as operations, and task forces are assigned definite objectives. The organization has been overhauled from top to bottom in order to make each unit a self-sustaining subsystem and to make the lines of communication and control clear and responsive. We will consider only two early examples of systems approaches in action. Today almost all military operations are based upon sound system theory.

The Battle of Britain. The Battle of Britain was going badly in 1943. The Royal Air Force was unable to contend with the massive formations of fighters and bombers which shuttled regularly across the channel. In desperation the British government called upon the leading scientists and urged them to develop a solution to the grave problem. It is to their everlasting credit that they realized that their scientists were a resource for something other than developing equipment and materials. The scholars took a crash course in military tactics. They accumulated as much data as was available concerning the patterns of attack, the tactics and conditions of interception, and the detailed results of all previous engagements. They then developed probability tables which predicted the likely outcome of all possible encounters, including such variables as numerical odds, meteorological conditions, time of day, and flight patterns. From that moment on the R.A.F. swarmed to action when conditions were optimal and avoided encounters that were foredoomed to failure. The results are history. Never have so many owed so much to so few analysts.

The Berlin Airlift. The United States Air Force was well schooled in systems strategy at the time of the Berlin blockade. The narrow air channel into Berlin was the only available input source for the millions of tons of life-sustaining resources needed by the people of Berlin. The logistics of air traffic alone seemed insurmountable. Once again the meteorological and flight pattern variables added to the complexity of the situation. Similar problems existed at other connective links between United States supply sources and West Germany. Once more the probability curves were charted and a strategy was planned based on the best available alternative. In the end the Berlin Airlift accomplished what only a few systems analysts had envisioned as the highly probable result. Note again that the solution to the problem was worked out in simulation before operations were initiated.

CYBERNETICS

Steering the System

Norbert Wiener borrowed the Greek word for helmsman when he coined the term "cybernetics." The significance of this choice should become apparent in this brief explanation.

Cybernetics is the science of controlling a system by providing a means of feeding back information about the progress of operations to a regulator. The regulator is designed to correct deviations from specified performance. The controlling device may be a self-regulator, such as a thermostat, or it may be a person who receives information which he can compare to desired operational standards. Whether the regulator is an instrument or a person, its function is to steer the system so that it will perform as designed.

In order to qualify as a cybernetic device there are three functions which must be performed:

1. Detect the critical information. (Performed by a detector or sensor, such as a float used to gauge the depth of a liquid or a criterion test to measure achievement of performance objectives.)
2. Evaluate the information to obtain a measurement which can be compared to specifications. (The gasoline gauge, for example, or the criterion standard established for an achievement test.)
3. Regulate the system with the necessary corrective input. (A thermostat is either open or closed. When closed, an electrical circuit is completed which in effect asks, "more, more," until the specifications are satisfied. When a criterion standard test is passed the directions to the individual are "go on to the next unit.")

It is important that we identify cybernetics with a preconceived plan. The bush pilot who flies by the seat of his pants is not the kind of helmsman to which we refer, but an automatic pilot exemplifies the principle nicely. In the master plan for the system there must be an automatic or adjustable device for regulating the performance so that the system is programmed to function within specified limits.

The network which consists of a detector and regulator, or a detector and evaluator as described in Chapter One, is referred to as a feedback loop. This is a well chosen expression since critical information about system performance is fed back in a loop or circuit from the detector to the regulating device. There are usually many feedback loops in a complex system if it is well designed.

Can Cybernetics Be Applied to a Social System?

Anyone who is skeptical concerning the ability of applied cybernetics to control social systems need only study carefully the strategy of political regulation as it is achieved in communistic countries where the regulation of people by information control is a calculated science. Edward Haskell and Harold Cassidy have revealed the cybernetic strategy of communistic indoctrination in *Plain Truth and Redirection of the Cold War*.[3] They demonstrated convincingly that strong information feedback networks are capable not only of rigid control of their own system but also of influencing competing systems. The authors stress that cybernetics is neutral where values are concerned with the potential to do either good or harm.

Marshall McCluhan has awakened us to the power of the medium which carries the message. His claim that the medium is the message is probably more dramatic than accurate, but we will never again discount the strong influence which the medium has on the message after reading McLuhan. Television is a cool medium which forces the viewer to become involved with the creation of the message while print is a hot medium with "uniform patterns and fast lineal movement." The cybernetic network, when thought of as a medium, binds the participant in control and conformity. Whether we use systems or are used by them, it is useful to be aware that what is happening is being caused to happen.

PERT:

A Management Technique

If you were to ask the typical manager what a systems approach is, he would more than likely describe one or more management techniques. In all probability, performance objectives, PPBS, and PERT would be mentioned. By this time it should be obvious that these techniques fall far short of a systems approach and in fact are only tools of systems management.

A systems approach must be directed toward a stated goal, objectives must be stated, and a solution strategy must be developed. Considerations of alternatives and constraints should occur at each step. Evaluation should be built into the planning so that the resulting system is responsive to management control. If *all* of these elements are not present, the application in question is not a systems approach.

---

[3] Edward F. Haskell and Harold G. Cassidy, *Plain Truth and Redirection of the Cold War*, (Private manuscript, 1961).

We have selected one of these techniques—planning, evaluation, and review technique or PERT—to illustrate this point. PERT is a useful management tool. Several PERT charts are used in Chapter Six to lay out a work breakdown schedule for establishing a learning disabilities program. In this chapter, a PERT schedule which was used to guide a team of teachers who were writing an individualized math program for the intermediate grades is presented. Unless PERT and other management techniques are surrounded by all of the functions and tasks of a systems approach, however, it will be a meaningless activity which is unresponsive to the objectives of the organization.

PERT and CPM Networks

The program, evaluation, and review technique (PERT) and the critical path method (CPM) will be treated as one and the same. Although there were significant differences at one time, each approach has come to take on the capability of the other until it is now not worthwhile to differentiate between them. Through this presentation, PERT will be used to designate this management technique.

Wherever there are critical schedule problems of considerable complexity involving factors of time, cost, or size, PERT should be considered. Here is how it works:

1. Take each operational objective and outline in time sequence order the tasks which must be accomplished in order to achieve it.
2. On a flow chart indicate the anticipated elapsed time for performing each task and identify those tasks which are to be performed simultaneously. Identify as *critical paths* any tasks which consume time while simultaneous tasks stand and wait.
3. Revise the flow chart based on a reallocation of resources in order to reduce the estimated time for critical paths, and also for adjustment of other inefficient procedures by substitution of alternatives.
4. Compare planned performance with actual performance.
5. Continuously review performance in order to improve efficiency.

The first three steps of this procedure are the *planning* stage, step four is *evaluation,* and step five is *review.* Step one is used extensively in business and industry and is referred to as a work breakdown schedule (WBS). It should be obvious by this time that all five steps would be necessary if this technique were to be used in a systems approach.

Garlock has listed the benefits which can be derived from PERT techniques. The benefits to educational managers from using PERT for such programs as curriculum development and educational research include:

1. A single network portrayal of the complete system.
2. A basis for a unified standard of communication among staff members.
3. A procedure that enhances common understanding at all decision making levels.
4. Reports that allow for thorough assessment of the sequence of activities, schedules, and costs.
5. Reports that assist in analyzing and evaluating the status of completed schedules and costs.
6. Reports that assist in forecasting or isolating potential problems in decision making.
7. Reports that assist in planning the best possible use of resources to achieve desired goals.
8. A means whereby all tasks must be specifically defined.
9. A means to determine where resources should be applied to determine the desired objectives.
10. A means to assist in identifying those areas of potential delays.[4]

PERT applications are appropriate for such problems as:

1. Long range curriculum development. (Scheduling the order in which course of study revision should occur, and assignment of personnel and financial resources by priority.)
2. Administrative council planning. (Scheduling the long range agenda and the calendar controlled activities of studies and reports.)
3. Facilities planning. (Keeping a visual chart of the long range plan for allocation of facilities and resources to enrollment groups.)
4. School board planning. (Scheduling the long range agenda and meeting calendar requirements.)
5. Opening and closing school. (Designing a system-wide schedule for opening and closing school each year.)
6. Individualizing instruction. (Designing individually prescribed instructional paths and controlling the flow of instructional materials.)

PERT Applied to a Summer Curriculum Project

In the summer of 1970 a team of teachers in Farmington, Connecticut were hired to develop an individualized instructional program for elementary school mathematics. There were many tasks to be performed in a six week period and it was obvious that the sequencing and timing of the tasks were critical since many of the tasks would have to be done individually. All of the tasks were written down as they were identified and listed on the work breakdown schedule in Figure 11. At this point it was not

---

[4] Jerry C. Garlock "PERT: A Technique for Education — Research in Review." *(Educational Leadership.* January 1968) p. 353.

necessary to consider sequence. When the list was completed, the tasks were analyzed in terms of the order in which they needed to be accomplished and the time in which series of tasks should be completed if the project were to be completed in the allotted time. The tasks were finally ordered on a time chart as presented in Figure 12 which is a PERT chart of the project. With the PERT available, the team members were able to coordinate their efforts and gauge their progress toward the goal.

Figure 11
Work Breakdown Schedule of Tasks to Be Performed by Mathematics Writing Team to Develop a Program of Individualized Study K-8

Math Contract K-8 7/70

Work Breakdown Schedule

1. Adopt a system for classifying mathematical concepts.

2. Identify performance objectives.

3. Write objectives in performance terms and code each objective. Ex. (31-425).

4. Write each objective *for the student.*

5. Develop a challenge test as a pretest for each performance objective. This should be an exact measure of the stated performance with the criterion standard made explicit. ($\%$ correct)

6. Develop a format for the student contract which includes the learner's objective and the challenge test.

7. Develop a format and procedure for making the challenge test answers available to the student.

8. Investigate, select, and assign instructional resource materials for each performance objective.

9. Develop a format for a student prescription sheet for each performance objective.

10. Develop a set of two post-tests for each performance objective as alternative forms. (Same standards as for challenge test)

11. Investigate and select, or design, a suitable survey test to be used for placement and diagnosis.

12. Develop a course of study map which provides an efficient visual flowchart of progress in performance objectives and makes assignment to new objectives obvious.

13. Develop a cumulative record form for recording progress.

14. Plan a schedule for getting materials to the typist.

15. Develop a teachers manual to provide a quick and efficient orientation to the system for teachers.

Figure 12
PERT Chart Applied to Work Breakdown Schedule in Figure 11

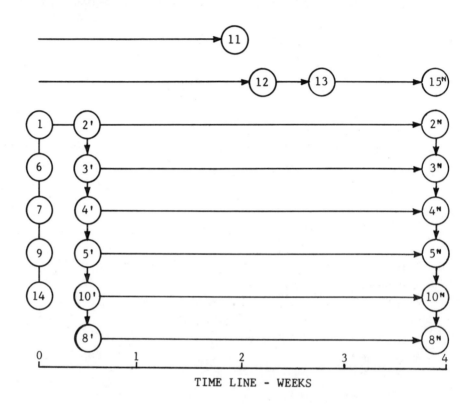

TIME LINE - WEEKS

SUMMARY

Management control was described as a procedure which helps the manager to detect and evaluate how well the organization is gaining its objectives. Progress is detected by observation or by automatic devices and fed to an evaluator which compares progress to standards and makes judgments. The major function of systems management is to place the administrator in a position where information about the system is directed to him so that deviations from the intended performance can be corrected immediately.

Automation was explained in relation to a system by describing it as a method of keeping the system goal-oriented by controlling what is happening automatically or by feeding back information about progress.

Automation is accomplished by conceptualizing how a system should behave and then making that behavior responsive to planning.

Systems were described as conceptual structures invented by man to help him understand interrelated activities. Systems do not exist in nature but are created as mental models to help us talk about interrelated functions or work with them. When we bring everything that is related to our goal together and perceive a system, we are in a much better position to control what is happening.

Cybernetics is the way a system controls its functioning by automatically correcting deviations. School administrators can become "controllers" by placing themselves in high-leverage positions where they can detect, evaluate, and control progress toward objectives.

PERT is a management technique which is used to analyze all of the activities which need to be accomplished in order to reach the objective and charting on a time line the order and time in which they should occur.

Of all of the systems with which school administrators must deal, the most important is the instructional system. We seldom look upon curriculum as a structure, but until this is done there is no way of managing instruction. Some educators will argue that instruction should not be managed because it is a creative process sensitive to individual needs and changing conditions. If a teacher knows what he is trying to do he has an objective in which case the systems approach can be helpful in discussing teaching strategies and evaluation procedures. Rather than working counter to humanistic teaching, the systems approach can be utilized to stipulate humanism and direct effort to its attainment. With this assurance, we can direct our attention in the next chapter to instruction as a system.

Developing an Instructional System

Chapter Three will assist the school administrator:

... to link classroom performance to the goals of education by establishing a chain of objectives and regulations extending through each authority level.

... to write organizational goals in a format which specifies what is to be accomplished.

... to write program objectives and performance objectives to specifications.

... to list three advantages to establishing a hierarchical approach to stating objectives.

... to cite at least six reasons why program objectives are beneficial to instruction.

... to cite at least six advantages to having performance objectives available.

... to describe orally why it is advantageous to think of a course of study as a structure.

... to describe the kind of testing program which must be developed to support a systems approach.

In this chapter we will deal with instructional systems in a straightforward manner using flowchart models and structural outlines. There is no intention to represent the instructional process as a simple system since it is certainly more complex than the most intricate rocketry system. While we are forced to simplify instruction at this time in order to construct models of what is happening, we will pay proper respect to complexities in later chapters.

In Chapter One we identified the three operations of a systems approach as: analyzing what needs to be done, designing the system, and managing the system. It is important that we always keep in mind the hierarchical level which is being considered when we refer to any of these operations. Let us consider the first operation, analyzing what needs to be done, or purpose. Some of the terms which are in current usage relating to purpose are goals of education, performance objectives, behavioral objectives, instructional objectives, and curricular goals. It is very seldom that these various goals and objectives are related to a hierarchy, yet it is essential that this be done if we are to eliminate the confusion caused by these loosely defined terms. In establishing operational definitions, the choice of terms is based on a rationale which will be developed throughout this chapter.

The purpose of education can be considered at many different levels:

1. The goals of society.
2. The goals of an educational institution.
3. Program objectives. (The social studies)
4. Course of study objectives. (U.S. History)
5. Unit of study objectives. (The Colonial Period)
6. Lesson plan objectives. (The daily lesson)

Even though this list considers more levels of instruction than most, other levels could be added if necessary. We could have, for example, established curriculum objectives for the humanities, and department objectives for a history department. Certainly in large schools where each of these hierarchial levels exists, it is necessary to consider the objectives for each of these distinct and often autonomous levels.

In this chapter we will consider three major instructional levels. This is necessary in order to simplify this text and is justifiable since three distinct levels can be logically identified as follows:

I. Educational Goals (Societal and institutional)
II. Program objectives[1] (Curriculum or course of study)
III. Performance objectives (Unit of instruction)

---

[1] Program objectives and performance objectives, related to instruction, may be either terminal or enabling objectives as distinguished in Chapter One. Because of this inconsistency we will always use the terms program objectives and performance objectives when dealing with instruction.

So far we have been considering only the first operation which is the
purpose of education. We can now add the second and third operations
which will be referred to as *structure* and *process*. A matrix layout illustrates how these distinctions are made.

Figure 13
The Operations of an Instruction System at Three Hierarchial Levels (Matrix)

	PURPOSE	STRUCTURE	PROCESS
Goal Level (I)	Educational goals	Organizational structure	Process decisions
Program Level (II)	Program objectives	Program structure	Instructional strategies
Performance Level (III)	Performance objectives	Unit of instruction	Instructional tactics

There is an appeal from many for a flow chart model which serves as a
model to aid conceptualization. The human mind strives for a gestalt in
order to provide meaning to interrelationships. *A flow chart is most
helpful when there are three dimensions to the matrix.* Since Figure 13
falls in this category, a flow chart may be helpful.

Our flow chart model allows us to add evaluation to our schema. In
Chapter One it was pointed out that it is mechanistic thinking to consider
evaluation as a separate operation since it must be an intergral part of all
operations. In Figure 14 we can see clearly that evaluation of the three
structural levels is responsive to the unique purpose of each level as
indicated by the broken line feedback arrows. Evaluation of the three
process levels must be responsive to both management control and
purpose at each hierarchic level.

It should be apparent that it makes no sense to write performance
objectives without reference to both program objectives and educational
goals. In actual practice, however, this is taking place every day because
these higher purposes are either not available or are stated in such a way
that they do not have relevance for performance. Clearly then, *both program objectives and educational goals must provide some direction for
performance or behavior if they are to be useful.* In this chapter we will
learn how to state these higher purposes so that they do provide direction
for performance at the contact level.

The same logic applies to the other areas of this tripartition. The unit of instruction must be organically related to the program structure. Process decisions set the stage for instructional strategies. Each lower level is totally dependent upon higher levels, while each higher level in turn provides the rationale and direction for lower levels.

Figure 14
The Operations of an Instructional System at Three Hierarchial Levels (Flow Chart Model)

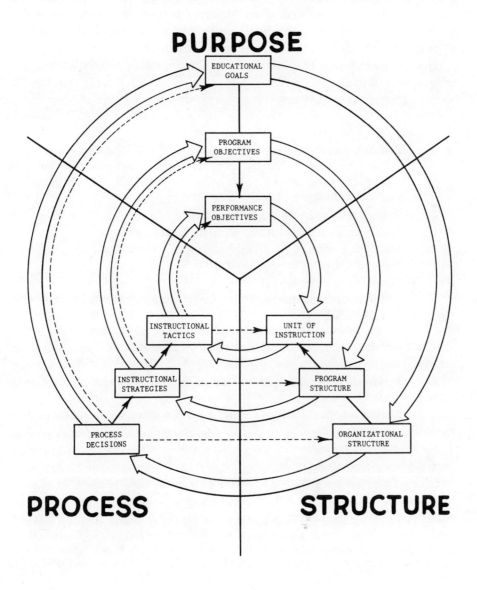

THE PURPOSE OF EDUCATION

The purpose of education is to provide enriched learning experiences in order to bring about desired change. When an educational organization is functioning effectively each operational level of the organization, from the board of education to the classroom teacher, knows exactly what performance is expected. Our commitment to education must be consistent, from the highest goals of our society to the objectives of a classroom lesson. At each operational level we must formulate statements which indicate desired performance. Each lower level must commit itself to a set of objectives which implement these goal statements.

The following outline indicates the performance commitment, the unique function, and the statement of purpose of each operational level in an educational organization:[2]

I. Society

Performance commitment–Cultural values and educational beliefs.

Unique function–Makes the ultimate decision concerning the purpose of education.

Statement of purpose–Goals of Society.

II. Board of Education (Board of Directors)

Performance commitment–To attain the goals of society.

Unique function–Formulates the purpose of the organization.

Statement of purpose–Organizational goals.

III. Superintendent (President)

Performance commitment–To implement the policy organizational goals of the board.

Unique function–Formulates the procedures of the organization.

Statement of purpose–Superintendent's regulations.[3]

IV. Middle Managers (Administrative Council)

Performance commitment–To implement the regulations of the superintendent.

Unique function–Identify the methods and means of achieving the program objectives.

Statement of purpose–Program objectives for courses of study.

V. Curriculum Manager

Performance commitment–To implement the program objectives.

---

[2] See Appendix A for a practical illustration as used in a Connecticut town.

[3] Appendix C presents a complete list of superintendent's regulations written to support the organizational goals adopted by the Board of Education in Farmington, Connecticut, in June 1970.

Unique function—Identify the methods and means of achieving the program objectives.

Statement of purpose—Program objectives for units of study. Performance objectives for daily lessons.

The Advantages of a Hierarchical Commitment of Performance

When the various operational levels are organized and operated on the basis of a clear-cut commitment and specific performance objective, the following advantages accrue:

1. Each level is responsive to higher levels and must establish objectives which indicate desired performance for lower levels.
   (a) The levels described are levels of responsibility. This does not preclude the possibility of agents from lower levels serving as advisors to higher agencies.
   (b) At any level, decisions about enabling procedures or methods and means of implementation should not be so prescriptive as to preempt the decisions of lower levels.
2. The performance expectations for each level are made explicit.
3. The commitment of immediate superiors is clear and concise and therefore provides strength and support to lower levels of authority.
4. Since the objectives are clearly stated at all levels, the entire system is open to honest inquiry.

Societal Goals

In our society the goals of education are not available in proclamation form. It has been left to organizations and individuals to analyze the desires of a democratic society and then to formulate what seems to be the goals of society. A unique study of the goals of education was published in *Goals for Public Education in Texas.*[4] Fourteen major historical contributions to goal analysis including the Committee of Ten (1893), American Youth Commission (1936), the Imperative Needs of Youth (1944), and the Commission on the Imperatives in Education (1966), were examined. Goals were also extracted from the statutes of the State of Texas, and many other state sources. The goal statements of four states were chosen as representative: Maryland, Pennsylvania, Massachusetts, and Oregon.

The goals from all these sources were laid out on a matrix and it was

---

[4]*Goals for Public Education in Texas.* (Texas: A Report by the Subcommittee on Goals to the Governor's Committee on Public Education 1969).

found that they could be classified in six columns. These six columns in turn were formulated as six major goals of education. This list is presented as the best available outline of educational goals and can serve as a point of departure for goal development.

1. Intellectual Discipline
2. Economic and Vocational Competence
3. Citizenship and Civic Responsibility
4. Competence in Human and Social Relations
5. Moral and Ethical Values
6. Self-Realization and Mental and Physical Health

A full development of these goals is presented in Appendix B. These societal goals are considered to be value positions held by society which have relevance for performance. They can be modified, extended, or refined, but in the final analysis a list similar to this provides a basis for determining the goals which are dictated by our cultural values and beliefs and the expected benefits which society appears to desire. Societal goals are an interpretation of cultural values and should be presented to society for acceptance.

Formulating societal goals. A formulation of a societal goal should meet the following requirements:

1. The purpose toward which the commitment is made should be clearly stated.
2. The statement should have relevance for performance.
3. The statement should not prescribe methods or means by which the goal is to be attained. (Exception: "Process goals," which will be discussed later.)

Examples of a societal Goal: The public schools should assist in the development of moral and spiritual values, ethical standards of conduct, and basic integrity.

Organizational Goals

Organizations are created to achieve the goals of society. They receive their authorization from society and must be responsive to society's demands. Organizations are a function of societal goals and provide the agency for accomplishing the desired performance. The essential role of an organization is to provide the management control necessary to attain societal goals. A formulation of organizational goals should meet the following requirements:

1. Each societal goal should be expanded by a phrase which specifies how this

will be accomplished. (Useful phrase introductions are "by providing...," "by defining...," "by promoting...")
2. The statement should be supported by a rationale which will explain why the performance is desirable.
3. The statement may incorporate an indication of the process to be used if the process itself is a major commitment of our society.

Example of an Organizational Goal: To assist each child in the development of moral and spiritual values, ethical standards of conduct, and basic integrity by establishing a learning environment in which each individual is encouraged to make ethical decisions and accepts the responsibility for his behavior.

Rationale: Moral and ethical values become meaningful to an individual when personal value judgments are solicited, providing the individual accepts the responsibility for his behavior.

The example cited is an instance where the process is prescribed. A decision has been made that spiritual values result from ethical judgments rather than from moralizing. In a democracy our concern for the individual learner makes it necessary to protect individual uniqueness from the de-personalization which might result from universal goal prescriptions.

Process goals — A special case. Performance implies an output which is a product. Many of the goals of education are product oriented. In a democratic society concerned with human rights, there is also a commitment to certain process goals based on process oriented values.

There are two major goals which represent a commitment to the individual learner. These process goals can be set up at two columns on a matrix so that each of the six societal goals can be modified by a statement which reflects the educational process necessary to be consistent with the values of a democratic society.

1. Each learner is a unique person. Programs should be established which take individual differences into account.
2. Learning how to learn may be as important as the learning itself.

The implication of this matrix is that each societal goal should include any modifying statements which are needed in order to be certain that the two process goals have been considered. This has been done in the example cited for organizational goals. If moral and spiritual values were the product to be attained, a set of values could be mandated and vigorously enforced. In deference to a judgment concerning learning how to learn in a free society, this was modified so that individuals can make their own ethical judgments under certain conditions.

Program Objectives

When the organization's goals are written to the standards described above, the managers of the system understand what their programs are supposed to accomplish. In an instructional system, program objectives are written for curricula and courses of study. Program objectives can be established for any instructional project including those which cut across the lines of the disciplines. An outdoor education program would be an example of such a project. Program objectives are any objectives which are written to accomplish the purpose of the organization at the planning stage. Performance objectives take over at the level of action or contact and are in the domain of the teacher and learner at the moment of instructional encounter.

The distinction between program objectives and performance objectives is one which is usually not made. The terms instructional objectives, performance objectives, and behavioral objectives are used synonymously in most instances and refer to objectives written at any level. This would not be a problem except that performance objectives and program objectives (as defined in this book) have several unique and exclusive attributes which makes it confusing to treat them as a single concept. There is currently a debate raging between the merits of the Bloom[5] and Tyler[6] approach to objectives versus the Mager[7] and Gagné[8] application. This debate is rendered meaningless when it is realized that Bloom and Tyler are dealing essentially with programs while Mager and Gagné are more interested in performance at the level of instruction.

The unique and exclusive attributes of program objectives are:

1. Program objectives are written by curriculum specialists rather than by instructors. (It is acknowledged that an instructor may well qualify as a curriculum specialist.)
2. Program objectives are never written for the moment of instruction but rather for a curriculum or course of instruction.

---

[5] B.S. Bloom, M.D. Engelhart, E.J. Furst, W.H. Hill, and D.R. Kathwohl, *Taxonomy of Educational Objectives. Handbook I: Cognitive Domain.* (New York; McKay, 1956).

[6] Ralph Tyler and Jack Merwin, *Working Paper on Objectives* ECAPE publication (Ann Arbor, Michigan: Committee on Assessing the Progress of Education, 1969).

[7] Robert Mager, *Preparing Instructional Objectives,* (Palo Alto, Calif.:   Fearon Publishers, Inc., 1962).

[8] Robert Gagné, *The Conditions of Learning* (New York: Holt, Rinehart and Winston, Inc., 1965).

3. The major concern of program objectives is the kind of behavior which is expected as a long range outcome, such as what the learner will do in society as a result of the experience. It is considered demeaning to instructors to prescribe how they are to teach. In general, program objectives are concerned with outcomes while performance objectives deal with the means.

Advantages of program objectives. Once goals have been established, the foundation has been prepared for formulating program objectives. Let us now consider why it is beneficial to have program objectives for curricula, courses of study, and units of study.

PROGRAM OBJECTIVES

. . . link goals to performance.

. . . provide the criterion standard for evaluation.

. . . allow the instructional plan to be open to honest inquiry.

. . . provide a guide for selecting appropriate content.

. . . indicate the cognitive level at which instruction should occur.

. . . indicate desirable affective outcomes.

. . . specify the process of instruction when this is necessary.

. . . make clear to the instructor what is to be taught and to the learner what is to be learned.

. . . establish the guidelines for performance.

Writing program objectives. There are several well known sources for the format of program objectives, *The Taxonomy of Educational Objectives, Handbooks I and II,* by Bloom et al, and the various handbooks on objectives directed by Tyler for the National Assessment of Educational Progress. When program objectives are written, they should conform to certain criteria in order to provide continuity from goals to performance:

1. Program objectives must be directly responsive to the next higher level of program objectives in order to maintain a direct link to organizational goals.
2. When program objectives become methods to attain ends rather than end outcomes, the validity of the choice of any specific method should be open to honest inquiry. (The teaching of formal grammar is not an end but a means to an end. If our ultimate objective is to improve communication through more effective and efficient language patterns, we should be certain that the means selected represent the best available alternatives.)
3. Program objectives should provide guidelines which make clear the level of cognition, the nature of affective outcomes, and any commitment to process goals established by the school system.
4. Program objectives must be expressed in such a way that they are relevant to performance analysis. More specifically, they should indicate in a general way how the learner will need to behave in order to validate that he has learned.

EXAMPLES OF PROGRAM OBJECTIVES

Curriculum objective—one of the purposes of the social studies is to provide both real and simulated experiences in which discussion is focused on ethical decision making.

Course of study objectives—South America—during the year there should be many opportunities for the students to consider the social history of South America from the standpoint of the effects of governmental actions on people. At the conclusion of this course, the learner should approach new situations by asking: "What is really happening here?", "Is my source of information biased?", "Have human values been properly considered?", and "What other alternatives were available?"

Unit of study objective—Brazil—At the completion of this unit, the student should be able to demonstrate that he can approach a problem from the standpoint of the ethical decisions involved. He should be free from narrow bias, should consider the welfare of all human beings rather than a select group, should be able to identify other alternatives, and should demonstrate his ability to make decisions which indicate that he is operating from an ethical framework.

Performance Objectives

We can now talk about performance objectives as the conditions of learning which implement program objectives. When program objectives have been written to the criteria established in the preceding section, instructors will understand what they are supposed to accomplish. Performance objectives are the guidelines which are established as a specification of the means selected to achieve program ends. The availability of performance objectives provides the following advantages:

1. Program objectives are linked to performance.
2. Performance objectives make it easier to select instructional materials.
3. They provide the criteria for evaluation of instruction and assessment of learning.
4. They assist in the selection of appropriate content.
5. They can specify the cognitive level at which learning should occur.
6. They provide a standard for diagnosing and prescribing for individual needs.
7. Performance objectives can specify means for attaining affective outcomes.
8. They make clear at the moment of instruction what the learner is expected to learn.

Writing performance objectives. Writers such as Mager, Gagné, and Banathy are very explicit in describing the conditions under which learning should occur, and the criterion for acceptable performance. In Chapter

One Mager's specifications for instructional objectives were presented. Banathy[9] has added further to Mager's outline:

A statement of objectives should specify:

1. *What* the learner is expected to be able to do by:
   (a) Using verbs that denote observable action.
   (b) Indicating the stimulus that is to evoke the behavior of the learner.
   (c) Specifying resources (objects) to be used by the learner and persons with whom the learner should interact.
2. *How well* the behavior is expected to be performed by identifying:
   (a) Accuracy of correctness of response.
   (b) Response length, speed, rate, and so forth.
3. *Under what circumstances* the learner is expected to perform by specifying:
   (a) Physical or situational circumstances.
   (b) Psychological conditions.

There is little more that can be said about writing performance objectives. What is obvious is that the degree of specification is too detailed for program objectives. Mager and Banathy are clearly dealing with a performance level.

EXAMPLES OF PERFORMANCE OBJECTIVES

(The numbers in parenthesis refer back to Banathy's outline.)

1. On a written objective test (3) the student will identify ten statements which describe Juan Peron's major attributes as: probable fact, personal opinion, or prejudiced judgment. (1) Eight correct answers will indicate satisfactory understanding. (2)
2. When confronted with a series of problems involving ethical judgments. (3) the student will demonstrate: that he gives proper concern to the effects of a given action on everyone involved, that he considers several alternatives, and that his decision is based on ethical considerations. (1) The student should rate at least satisfactory on a five point scale rated by the instructor on which a satisfactory rating is three. (2)

Answering Objections to Objectives

Some educators object to stating instructional objectives in performance terms. Some of these objections are based on misinformation, some

---

[9] Bela H. Banathy, *Instructional Systems,* (Palo Alto, California: Fearon Publishers, 1968) p. 33.

are partly true, and a few seem to be valid. These objections will be presented along with a response to each.

1. Affective outcomes are apt to be overlooked because they are difficult to express in behavioral terms. *Response*—Most advocates of instructional objectives pay considerable attention to affective outcomes. Actually they are not difficult to state as Krathwohl and Bloom were able to demonstrate in their second handbook which dealt exclusively with educational objectives in the affective domain. What is difficult is the evaluation of these objectives, but that should not stop us from writing affective outcomes and teaching with these objectives in mind.
2. Performance objectives are usually trite. *Response*—There are numerous examples of performance objectives which are of major importance. If a list of objectives seems to be trite it may be that low level cognitive objectives are being stressed to the neglect of higher cognitive processes and affective outcomes. In this case performance objectives have served the commendable function of casting the spotlight on the meager instructional fare.
3. Objectives emphasize short term outcomes. *Response*—Objectives emphasize whatever you want them to. They can describe behavior which should occur at year's end or ten years from now.
4. Objectives are too prescriptive in terms of the methods and means of teaching; they tend to restrict a creative teacher. *Response*—This is certainly possible. If this happens at least the battle lines are clearly drawn. One of the virtues of stating objectives is that they are open to inquiry. Go ahead and challenge objectives which are too prescriptive!
5. Performance objectives attempt to turn a teacher into a programmed instructor. *Response*—At the level of the daily lesson the teacher should determine his own performance objectives. No teacher should program himself rigidly or allow anyone else to program him.

Proceed with Caution

It is not our intention to imply that a well written objective is all that is required to guarantee that instruction is properly directed. Objectives should not be accepted on the basis of form alone. It is possible for performance objectives to meet all of Banathy's specifications and yet be archaic, inconsequential, biased, or even stupid. When you take on someone else's objectives wholesale—"let the buyer beware." Here are some other precautions:

1. At times program objectives deal with means rather than ends. For example, an objective of a U.S. History course might be: At the completion of this course the student should be able to trace the chronological development of American history citing at least three examples of political, economic, and military events for each fifty year period, with 85% accuracy.

This objective is clearly someone's interpretation of how young people acquire an understanding and appreciation of their heritage. This is a means to an end objective rather than an end in itself. All enabling objectives should be put to a severe test of relevancy before they are accepted.

2. There is a tendency to look ahead to evaluation and to settle for objectives which can be easily measured. The result of this will be that low level cognitive objectives will predominate. The lack of readily available measurement devices should not be allowed to interfere with the writing of objectives.

3. If performance objectives are equated with product there will be a tendency to deal with product objectives to the exclusion of process. If the objective is to promote the inquiry process through the vehicle of science content, the performance objective should focus on inquiry and not science.

When Teachers Write Objectives

There is more confusion and disagreement about formulating objectives at the level of daily instruction that at any other stage; this is the point at which the teacher should be writing his own objectives. When a curriculum study group starts writing objectives below the level of the unit, they are taking on a task which is both unnecessary and unwise. It is unfortunate that our best examples of objective writing come from programmed instruction because it is necessary to deal with step-by-step procedures in this mode of instruction. This conveys the impression that this is the procedure which is also best for teacher mediated instruction. Most of the programmed instruction is directed to training rather than teaching, therefore it would be unwise to use it as a model for anything but training activity.

There has been considerable discussion concerning whether or not teachers should write performance objectives for daily lessons. Some of the more common reservations which teachers express are:

1. I know what my objectives are and it would be a waste of time to write them down.

2. My objectives are primarily in the affective domain and cannot be stated in performance terms.

3. I am a creative person and often operate by intuition. Performance objectives would shackle my creativity.

The general answer to these reservations would be that unless behavioral change in pupils is occurring, no learning is taking place. In this context attitudes and appreciations would be considered as behavior. From this standpoint we can answer each of the objections. In response to the first reservation we must hold that the objectives must be available for honest inquiry. This means that the teacher, the learner, and the observer should all know what the teacher expects to happen. If the teacher is able to communicate her objectives in some way other than writing them this could be acceptable. At this time it is difficult to know what these acceptable alternatives might be. The second reservation must be rejected on the basis of ample evidence that objectives in the affective domain can be written. The final reservation can be considered with sympathy. There are certainly many teachers who function very effectively in this manner. The flaw in this position is that it is possible to write objectives which state clearly that an inquiry approach will be used or that methods and means will be selected as needed. It is understandable that the instructor might feel that he doesn't know how he will accomplish his objectives, but it would be ludicrous to hold that he doesn't know what his objective is. The most permissive, creative, or intuitive approach conceived must be directed to some purpose or the learning which might occur will not be responsive to the needs of the learner.

THE STRUCTURE OF LEARNING

> The idea of a system of instruction is as intriguing and fashionable as the concept of the structure of an academic discipline and we are about at the same point in characterizing instruction as systematic as we are in describing a subject as structured. It is one thing to accept these concepts in abstract form and quite another actually to probe what we teach to determine its structure or analyze what we do to discover its system.[10]

If we cannot conceptualize a structure for an academic discipline, we will find it impossible to develop an instructional system. Fortunately there have been significant developments in the past few years which have served to give impetus to the development of structures of learning. Bruner stated the need for structure quite clearly in *The Process of Education.*[11]

> To learn structure, in short is to learn how things are related... The approach taken is a practical one. Students, perforce, have a limited exposure to the materials they are to learn. How can this exposure be made to count in their thinking for the rest of their lives? The dominant view among men who have been engaged in preparing and teaching new cur-

---

[10] John B. Haney et al, "Reply to Questions about Systems," (Audiovisual Instruction, May, 1965) p. 369.

[11] Jerome Bruner, *The Process of Education.* (Cambridge: Harvard University Press, 1960) pp. 7, 11-12.

ricula is that the answer to this question lies in giving students an understanding of the fundamental structure of whatever subjects we chose to teach. This is a minimum requirement for using knowledge, for bringing it to bear on problems and events one encounters outside the classroom—or in classrooms one enters later in one's training. The teaching and learning of structure, rather than simply the mastery of facts and techniques, is at the center of the problem of transfer. There are many things that go into learning of this kind, not the least of which are supporting habits and skills that make use of the materials one has come to understand. If the earlier learning is to render later learning easier, it must do so by providing a general picture in terms of which the relations between things encountered earlier and later are made as clear as possible.

Bruner has made an eloquent plea for the type of teaching which allows the student to discover the fundamental structure of a subject. A great deal of work has been devoted to developing such meaningful structures by specialists within the disciplines.

By virtue of its existence, every curriculum has a structure. Social studies has traditionally been built around an accumulation of facts and generalizations. A new science program is built entirely on a mode of inquiry. A recent secondary social studies program is developed on a problem solving technique. A modern math program is constructed around a hierarchical learning sequence.

The problem with many of these structures is that they do not provide the power of consolidation of knowledge or a frame of reference which helps things to hang together in a meaningful interrelationship. Bruner urged that "the curriculum of a subject should be determined by the most fundamental understanding that can be achieved of the underlying principles that give structure to that subject." [12]

Curriculum Structure and Instructional Systems

In order for a system to function to its potential, it must be considered as an organic unit in which all sets of interrelationships are organized for efficient and effective operation. *The greater the organizing power of the key concepts, the more powerful is the system.* For this reason, old courses of study which are nothing more than catalogs of classification and description are poor fare for a systems approach. They are similar to the mechanical operations of pre-automated technology which are so obvious that straight linear thinking was all that was demanded in order to understand them.

---

[12] Jerome Bruner, *The Process of Education.* p. 31.

There are newer approaches to structuring a curriculum which seem to fall into the same category as the old data catalogs. The search for generalizations in the field of social studies which was directed by Paul Hanna[13] uncovered 3272 generalizations. Obviously there is no organizational power in such an overpowering number, even though they were grouped into nine basic activities of men.[14]

Gagné[15] approaches structure by looking at learning in terms of the logical sequence in which it should occur. He suggests a sequence which begins with stimulus-response, and continues through chaining, verbal association, multiple discrimination, concept learning, principle learning, and terminates with problem solving. From a structure building standpoint, one would start with a set of important problems and determine the prerequisite learnings which were necessary. The danger of using Gagné's approach to structuring is that the sum total of his learning chains would be accepted as the structure. This is a very mechanistic approach and has no power of organization to recommend it.

Fortunately there has been some significant work on structure done in recent years. Figure 15 reproduces the efforts of Lawrence Senesh who has developed a conceptual structure for economics based on key concepts and essential interrelationships.[16] An outline such as this seems to provide a structure within which principles, concepts, and other content will hold together. Experts in the discipline are in a position to improve the structure since it is now open to inquiry. Similar structures are presented in the same article for political science, anthropology, sociology, and geography.

---

[13] Paul R. Hanna and John R. Lee, "Generalization from the Social Sciences," *Social Studies in the Elementary Schools,* Thirty-Second Yearbook of the National Council for the Social Studies (Washington, D.C., 1962) pp. 71-75.

[14] The nine basic activities cited by Hanna are: educating; providing recreation; protecting and conserving; organizing and governing; expressing esthetic and spiritual needs; creating new tools and techniques: producing, exchanging, and distributing; transporting; and communicating.

[15] Gagné, *The Conditions of Learning.*

[16] Lawrence Senesh, *Organizing a Curriculum Around Social Studies: Concepts in Structure in the Social Studies.* (Washington, D.C.: National Education Association 1968) p. 62.

Figure 15
Fundamental Ideas of Economics

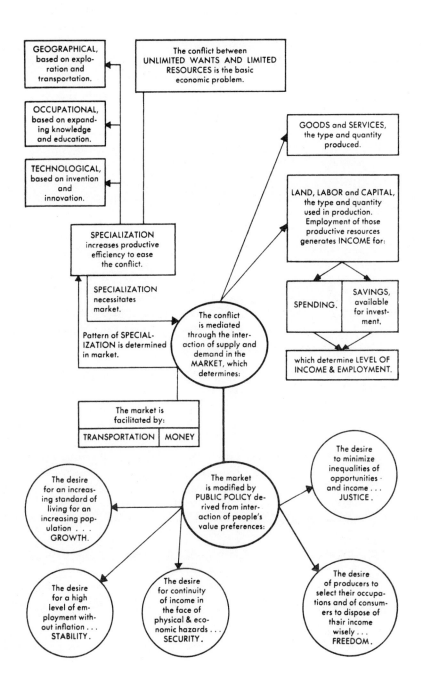

Designing an Instructional System

Once the structure of the curriculum has been established, we can consider the problem of designing an instructional system within this conceptualization. All decisions related to design must be made with direct reference to the program objectives. We are now ready to select the methods—means which is the systems design operation. The following decisions will have to be made based on the alternatives which are available:

1. What is the sequence of learning?
2. At what cognitive level will learning occur?
3. At what affective level will learning occur?
4. How will the learner be motivated?
5. How will learning be evaluated?

Designing the sequence of learning. If learning is to be meaningful all of the prerequisite conditions to learning must have been mastered by the learner. The work of Gagné should be referred to for a full treatment of these conditions.[17] The implication of this sequence is that the designer must establish a sequence of input which will guarantee that the learner will proceed through the sequence, unless it can be reliably determined that he has already made some progress in this direction.

1. *Stimulus-response learning.* The learner can make a specific response to a given stimulus.
   Example: Science. The learner can perform all of the necessary motor skills such as handling equipment. He is familiar with the names of all common objects which will be used.
   Implications for teaching: The teacher will have available a list of skills and abilities which may have to be reinforced by stimulus-response.
2. *Chaining.* The learner can make a meaningful connection between related sets of stimulus—response items (both motor skill and verbal chains) or can recall sequences of named objects.
   Implications for teaching: The teacher will have available a list of stimulus—response links which are needed by the learner. Reinforcement through prompting and repetition may be necessary.
3. *Multiple discrimination.* The learner is able to make accurate associations of stimulus and response even when the stimuli are in many respects similar.
   Example: Science. The learner can collect together objects which have a common attribute.
   Implications for teaching: The teacher must present stimuli in a manner

---

[17] Gagné, *The Conditions of Learning.*

which emphasizes the attribute to be distinguished. Repetition and reinforcement may be necessary.

4. *Concept learning.* The learner can identify the common attribute of a class of stimuli that differ widely in appearance.

   Example: Science. The learner can make judgments which enable him to identify new objects in terms of a concept and will expand the universe of experiences which belong to the concept.

   Implications for teaching: The teacher must be able to present a number of stimuli which represent the concept in order to aid the learner in concept growth.

5. *Principle learning.* The learner is able to make a cause-effect connection between two or more concepts.

   Example: Science. The movement of the shorter arm of a Class I lever imparts motion to an object that is greater in amount, smaller in force, and opposite in direction.

   Implications for teaching: Present the related concepts. Either allow the learner to discover the principle if the process of learning is inquiry, or describe the principle involved.

6. *Problem solving.* The learner is able to combine two or more principles to solve a problem.

   Example: Science. Based on his observations, the learner can state what makes plants grow.

   Implications for teaching: The teacher must provide the materials or the situations which are conducive to problem solving. The teacher can guide the thinking process but should not state the principle to be attained.

This necessarily brief treatment of an important consideration in instructional design was extracted from Gagné's, *The Conditions of Learning.* The major part of this book is devoted to aspects of the sequence of instruction and will afford valuable insights for the reader who is interested in the full development of Gagné's theory.

Identifying the Cognitive Level at Which Learning Will Occur

It is important to know what is expected of the learner in terms of the cognitive level at which he is expected to function. Some writers differentiate between low level cognition such as sensing, recalling, and retrieving and all high level cognition such as analyzing, evaluating, and synthesizing. This distinction serves the purpose of directing the teacher to something other than low level cognition if this is the objective. The work of Bloom, et al[18] has become a classic in this area. The six taxonomic levels which

---

[18] Bloom et al, *A Taxonomy of Educational Objectives, Handbook I.*

they developed extend from low-level knowledge of the recall variety through evaluation which they consider to be the highest cognitive process.

1. *Knowledge* The recall of specifics or universals.
2. *Comprehension.* A low level of understanding. The object has meaning.
3. *Application.* A concept or principle has been abstracted and is available in the learner's mind in place of the direct experience.
4. *Analysis.* A breakdown of an organized understanding into elements with proper regard for the hierarchy of ideas involved and the important interrelationships which have occurred.
5. *Synthesis.* The putting together of elements so as to form a meaningful whole. This is a creative process in which the learner discovers and formulates the organizational principle.
6. *Evaluation.* The ability to make qualitative and quantitative independent judgments about the value of material, methods, or ideas.

The establishment of a hierarchy of cognitive processes makes it possible to form a link between the objectives and the output based on the cognitive level which is desired. If the program objectives express the desire that the learner should be able to synthesize from his experiences, it is clear that teaching and evaluation which are directed to simple recall are inappropriate.

Identifying the Affective Level at Which Learning Will Occur

Affective outcomes deal with interests, attitudes, appreciations, values, and emotions. Again Krathwohl and Bloom have provided a taxonomy which has been widely accepted. If our objectives are directed to affective outcomes, it is important that the teacher, the learner, and the observer have a more clear idea of the level of affective response which is desired. Krathwohl et al[19] developed five levels in their affective domain:

1. *Receiving.* Willing to pay attention.
2. *Responding.* Committing one's self by actively behaving in some way.
3. *Valuing.* A thing or a behavior has been taken on as an attitude or a belief.
4. *Organization.* One's values are organized into a system which has interrelationships and priorities.
5. *Characterizing.* Integration of attitudes, beliefs, and ideas into a philosophy which can be said to characterize one's point of view.

---

[19]David Krathwohl, Benjamin Bloom, and Bertram Masia, *Taxonomy of Educational Objectives. Handbook II: Affective Domain,* (New York: David McKay Company Inc. 1964).

We can now specify objectives in the affective domain much as we do in the cognitive area. Certainly there is far less exactness in this domain and evaluation procedures are rather primitive, but at least we have a procedure for stating objectives with a degree of specificity which has not been possible in the past.

Motivating the Learner

We have usually proceeded in designing instruction as though any procedure which is designed is intrinsically self-motivating. A great deal of work in the area of learning theory has served to dispel this myth. We now know that it is our obligation as designers to consider the learner and to build into the design techniques and procedures which will lure the learner to attend, comprehend, and even enjoy the instructional program. The following guidelines should be considered as means of attracting the learner:

1. Establish a clear rationale which clarifies for the learner why this particular learning is valuable.
2. Provide a means of feedback which informs the learner about his progress and steers him to appropriate material.
3. Guide the learner to develop his own standards of achievement and progress.
4. Guide the learner to recognize his learning style and develop his own learning strategy.
5. Capitalize on the intrinsic motivational value of discovery learning.

Evaluating the Learning

Evaluation is a straightforward process of feeding back information to the learner about his progress. The technical aspects of inserting detectors and evaluators into a management control system network were presented in Chapter Two and will not be duplicated here. If performance objectives have been written to conform to the standards outlined in this chapter, the criterion of acceptable performance has been established. The task which remains is to select measurement procedures and evaluative devices which allow us to assess progress.

We must recognize clearly that most of the tests which are now available to schools are not useful as evaluative devices in a systems approach. While we wait for this situation to be corrected we must design tests of our own which accomplish this purpose. These tests fall in the following categories:

1. *Survey tests.* Survey tests are broad assessments of a learner's status relative

to the structure of our instructional program. A survey test in history which is concerned with chronological facts is of no use in a structure designed toward major concepts and problem solving.

2. *Pre-tests.* The pre-test must accurately pinpoint where each individual is located on a learning continuum such as Gagné's, which proceeds from stimulus-response prerequisites to problem solving. A pre-test must be designed for a specific objective. It presumes that most learners do not have to start from step one and that some may even have achieved the objective before learning begins. When used as a readiness test, it may indicate that some learners are not ready for the unit of instruction contemplated.

3. *Mastery tests.* Mastery tests measure progress at any desired point against a standard. The test is established as criterion evidence that learning has occurred at a satisfactory level. Among specialists, this type of testing is becoming known as criterion testing.

4. *Post-test.* The post-test is also a mastery test but differs in that it measures the degree to which the objective has been attained. Since the objective should have indicated the conditions under which learning can be demonstrated as fulfilled, and the criterion gauge of success, a post-test must be designed to meet these standards. The term "summative testing" is being used to distinguish these end-of-unit or course tests.

There is a critical need for reformation in the field of tests and measurements. The efforts of educators who design their own tests and the commercial evaluators must be directed to the specific needs of systems evaluation. We can consider some of the factors which should be included in a testing program which is fully responsive to the needs of the classroom.

1. Mastery tests (criterion) should be designed primarily to provide feedback to the learner rather than to determine grades.

2. The use of techniques such as interviews and questionnaires should be investigated as alternatives to traditional testing with its proven limitations. Evaluation is a broader concept than measurement and we must look beyond quantifiable measures for assessing high-cognitive and affective objectives.

3. Research techniques are not appropriate for evaluating on-going instruction. We should insist that research procedures not be allowed to predetermine how progress is evaluated. Research and evaluation are distinctly different functions and it is time that we manage instruction accordingly.

4. Norms should be replaced by standards in many instances. Mastery tests should be based on criterion standards which in effect are absolute indicators that learning has occurred at a satisfactory level. Standards can be adjusted for individuals and they can also be changed as experience indicates. The determination of success in terms of placement within the scores of a group is useful for purposes of comparison but should be discontinued as a means of reporting progress in formative situations.

5. Evaluation has been concerned almost completely with *production* in instructional areas. Our educational objectives and evaluative procedures should devote considerably more attention to the *human development* of the learner.
6. Testing should be clearly related to the structure and sequence of instruction.

It would be appropriate to conclude this chapter with a section entitled *The Process of Education* since we have only covered two of the three areas of our instructional system. A theoretical treatment of this subject would extend beyond the purpose of this book and can be acquired in Bruner's classic of the same name. Our concern with the practical aspects of this topic can be deferred until Chapter Six, "Organizing a Learning Disabilities Program." This entire chapter deals with the third operation of a systems approach: manage the system.

We will now turn from theory to practice and examine several curricular areas in detail. Chapter Four will deal with all of the practical considerations of the first operation: analyze what needs to be done. The area of the curriculum to be considered is elementary school mathematics. Chapter Five, "Individualizing Instruction with a Systems Approach," is devoted to the second operation; design the system.

FOUR

Applying an Instructional System to Elementary School Mathematics

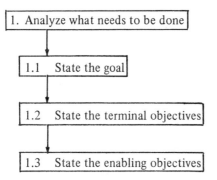

The first operation of a systems approach was presented in Chapter One and is summarized in the flow chart reproduced here. In this chapter we will apply this procedure to a problem which is becoming a serious concern for school administrators, developing a course of study. The illustrations and applications presented in this chapter will enable the administrator:

    ...   to outline the specific tasks to be performed in formulating the major goals of a course of study.

    ...   to write the major goals for a course of study in a format which provides direction for program objectives.

... to outline the specific tasks to be performed in preparing program and performance objectives for a course of study.

... to write program objectives and performance objectives for a course of study.

In this chapter we will apply a systems approach to curriculum revision in the elementary school. We will deal exclusively with the first operation; analyze what needs to be done. In this hypothetical study an outdated mathematics program will be analyzed in order to determine if a revision is necessary. All tasks of the first operation will be considered, but the primary purpose will be to state the goals and formulate the performance objectives. Almost any subject area could have been selected but elementary school mathematics was preferred since there is available some excellent work in the area of goals and objectives which will strengthen the practical aspect of this chapter.

FORMULATING THE GOALS OF MATHEMATICS

There must be a commitment to change by everyone who will be affected or seeds of dissension will be sown along with the anticipated improvements. It has been pointed out in Chapter One that it is the client who must formulate the goal while the analyst can only offer his assistance by suggesting proper procedures. In this case, the client is the superintendent of schools acting as the agent for the school board and the presumption must be made that the board, the teachers, and the public must be in agreement that a study of the present situation is necessary.

Is the Present Math Program Satisfactory?

In most cases, the curriculum analyst is invited in with not much more direction than, "We'd like to revise our math program and bring it up to date." Following the procedures established in Chapter One, the analyst would ask a series of questions designed to assess the present situation. All present problems or dissatisfactions may well be constraints to the new system unless they can be eliminated. On the other hand, if there are any procedures which are functioning well they would probably be retained as the least costly alternative if they were found to be consistent with the new goals and the revised performance objectives. In a larger complex organization the data would be collected in the form of reports, budgets, and questionnaires, but in this case a simple dialogue will be used to illustrate the procedure. (*A.* is the systems analyst and *C.* is the client.)

A. Do you have a course of study guide or any other written materials on elementary school mathematics?

C. Yes, but it won't help you. The teachers don't use it anymore.

A. How is math being taught now?

C. In three of our elementary schools they are using textbook X. Textbook Y is used in the other two schools. Both series are out of date.

A. In effect then, the textbook provides the course of study?

C. That's right.

A. Is there any ability grouping or individualized instruction?

C. Center School has homogeneous grouping in the intermediate grades. I don't know of any individualized instruction going on.

A. Are there any classrooms using programs which might be called modern?

C. Yes. Two rooms at Center are using the A program. It's a modern math program and the teachers are enthused about it.

A. Who is it that feels a change is necessary?

C. Well, I do. A few of the principals have been pushing for it, too. A couple of the school board members are aware of the fact that we are out of date and are beginning to ask for a change.

A. What about the public?

C. Well, a few parents have been reading about programs in other towns and are asking questions. I can't say that there's a big push, though.

A. And the teachers?

C. In general, I'd say that the teachers are interested in new ideas. Of course, we haven't taken a survey so I couldn't say what the consensus would be.

A. What would you say are the major reasons why a change should be made?

C. The main reason is that the present program isn't relevant to the needs of society in this day and age. We know that there has been a lot of work done in modern math and it isn't reflected here. We're not doing anything for either the slow learner or the bright student. We haven't even begun to consider individual differences. On top of that we aren't doing a good job of achieving our outdated goals. Not according to our achievement scores, anyway.

A. What factors are probably preventing you from achieving your outdated goals? (I.A.1b)

C. In the first place, no one knows what those goals are. We pretty much follow the textbook and hope that the goals are covered. I guess that the real goal is to do well on the achievement tests.

A. Do you have enough money in the budget to get the materials which you need for the present program?

C. Yes, I'd say so. Textbooks and workbooks, anyway. We haven't purchased new books because we don't want to perpetuate these programs.

A. Could I have a copy of each of the textbooks in use and the course of study guide? I'd like the teacher's editions if possible. I'd also like to see the achievement test results for the past five years.

C. No problem. I'll get them all for you.

On the basis of this simple dialogue, the systems analyst was able to discern what the present condition was in general. After studying the materials he called back for further information concerning teacher-pupil ratio, budget allocations for mathematics materials, teacher salaries, and performance standards for pupils.

Within a week's time the analyst returned to the superintendent's office with a questionnaire which he recommended be given to all teachers. He suggested that it would be helpful in assessing the present situation and would also serve to determine the extent to which the teachers were committed to making a change. On the basis of this information, the school board and the public would be informed that a study was under way. The superintendent deleted several items for which information was already available and agreed to send out the questionnaire over his signature.

ELEMENTARY MATHEMATICS QUESTIONNAIRE

1. On the basis of your own judgment as to the type of mathematics which our youngsters will need in their adult lives, and considering your familiarity with new directions in math which you have read about, how would you rate the mathematics program you are now using?

   _____ Very good   _____ Needs some improvement
   _____ Satisfactory   _____ Needs to be completely revised

2. How much time do you spend each day in direct teaching of mathematics? _____

3. Estimate how much time each day the average pupil devotes to mathematics including both directed teaching and seatwork. _____

4. On what basis would you decide that one of your pupils had not met the standard required for success? (Has mastered the course?)

5. Are there any programs or materials which you are familiar with which you feel would be an improvement over our present program?

6. List any college courses or in-service programs which you have had in modern mathematics.

7. If you have any comments which will aid in this study please present them here.

By combining the information previously collected with the questionnaire results the systems analyst was able to complete the first three tasks in the form of a brief summary:

> Present instructional materials are outdated. The teacher-pupil ratio is 30 to 1. There is no specific amount budgeted for mathematics but apparently ninety cents per pupil is expended for textbooks, workbooks, and supplies. The average teacher's salary is $11,130.
>
> Sixty-three percent of the teachers feel that a complete revision is needed. Eighteen percent favor some improvement. Six percent rated the present program as satisfactory and 5 percent rated it as very good. Only 7 percent of the teachers have had a course in modern mathematics and none have had in-service work. (123 teachers responded.)
>
> Although the schedule calls for 45 minutes of mathematics per day, the average teacher spends 36 minutes in direct teaching and 30 percent of the teachers spend only 30 minutes. Only 15 percent devoted the recommended 45 minutes to math. The average pupil spends 50 minutes per day in school working on math but there was a wide variation ranging from 30 minutes to 90 minutes. All teachers reported that mathematics is taught every day.
>
> The constraints to success in the present operation are: lack of clearly stated goals, absence of performance objectives, lack of commitment to an instructional process, and lack of a planned program of evaluation.
>
> There are no standards for measuring performance relative to objectives. Only 17 percent of the teachers indicated that their standards would depend upon the individual child. Work habits were cited as reasons for failure more frequently than were any form of standards of mastery. No teacher mentioned anything which resembled performance objectives as a guide for evaluation.
>
> The standard achievement scores indicate that four of the five schools are consistently performing at the level of the regional norms at all quartile levels. Porter School was consistently higher than the norms at the 75th percentile and slightly higher at the 50th percentile. There was no indication from the teachers that these scores played a role in assessment of performance, although they would have had to volunteer this information in answer to question five. Neither the school board nor the school administration has made any judgment concerning the level of performance of pupils, either on test performance or otherwise.

It should be noted that these reports are a straight non-judgmental summary of the present condition. It is not the task of the systems analyst to evaluate the present status but merely to help the client formulate his goal, and to gather any information which will be helpful later. There has been no value judgment made concerning the merits of modern math or individualized instruction, but only an attempt to see things as they are.

Describing the End Product

It is the client who must come up with the specifications for the end product. The analyst will assist by recommending various techniques for formulating goals which are relevant. He will also want to be certain that there is some indication of the expected performance since this will be the keystone around which the entire system will be built. In describing the end product, the client is in fact formulating the goal although it will be necessary to restate the description in precise goal terminology as task I.A.3.

Goal setting is actually a much more complicated task in a social situation than it would be for a business or military enterprise. *The goals of an educational institution must be responsive to the desires to society.* It would be beneficial if well-stated goals were readily available, but in this country there is a reluctance to establish goals because of our traditional disdain for imposed authority. With no clear goals available, each school district must determine what it feels are the desires of society. This is no simple task.

Goals for School Mathematics[1] is the best available source of goals for modern math. These goals were formulated by twenty-five outstanding mathematicians and psychologists in 1963. They are relevant to our automated society and also give adequate attention to the process of education as well as the product. Some of the goals presented would not be considered to be goals according to the definition provided in this book because they go further than stating the goals of society and actually prescribe the methods of achieving the goals. For example, one recommendation stated that the ideas of geometry should be taught in the elementary schools. This is actually a program objective since it prescribes content as the means to an end. Nowhere in this book were the goals stated in outline form, therefore it is necessary to read carefully to uncover them. A full reading is well worth the effort but here is an interpretation of how they might have appeared had they been presented in some organized fashion:

1. All young people should acquire the technical skills of mathematics. These skills should be interwoven into the acquisition of new concepts and not presented in isolation. (A process goal.)
2. Young people should learn the major concepts of mathematics. These concepts should be selected not because they are modern but because they have organizing power and therefore contribute the best learning structure.
3. Creative and independent mathematical thinking should be developed by means of a discovery approach. (A process goal.)

---

[1] *Goals for School Mathematics,* (Boston: Houghton Mifflin Company, 1963).

4. The concepts of mathematics and the sequence of technical skills should not be sacrificed if certain learners are slow to discover them on their own. Directed teaching should assure that these goals are attained. (Another process goal.)

Is the Contemplated Change the Best Alternative?

The systems analyst is not a decision-maker and can only bring forth data which assists the superintendent to make his judgment. When the specified changes have not been stated within the parameters presented in Appendix A it will be necessary to point out to the superintendent why the preparation for the goal formulation must meet certain requirements.

Whenever the client indicates in any way by what process the goal is to be attained (as in process goals of instruction), he has preempted the right of the systems designer and the manager to make process decisions which normally would be their function. If the superintendent has gone overboard in prescribing processes he should be reminded (gently, of course) that he is removing from consideration all other process alternatives, and considerably limiting the value of cost efficiency studies.

What Limits Are Imposed on Operation and Design?

The analyst must be certain that there is a clear understanding concerning the limits imposed by the client on operation and design. Following the procedure established in Chapter One a list of restrictions was compiled:

> *Operational Limits*—The same financial resources will be available for operating the new math program as are now available except that normal yearly increases will be prorated to mathematics. Forty-five minutes of teacher time and sixty minutes of pupil time will be available. The teacher-pupil ratio will remain the same. Funds will be available for conducting an in-service workshop. *Design Limits*—There are no advance restrictions placed on the methods and means of accomplishing objectives.

How Will Performance Be Measured?

The statements concerning desired change identify *what* is to be done. When we consider the performance measure for the desired outcome, we are seeking to indicate *how we can be certain that we have reached our goal.* In order to do this we must provide a precise indication of the kind of behavior or performance which can be accepted as evidence that the goal has been reached. We are interested in the performance which is present at the completion of a child's elementary education. It must be remembered that there will be a great deal of evaluation taking place relative to program objectives and performance objectives. This will be in the nature of regular and instant feedback which reports on progress in terms of objectives. There is obviously no need for the goal measures to attempt to duplicate this more detailed and specific evaluation. On the other hand, the attainment of performance and program objectives does not necessarily guarantee that the goals have been achieved. The discrepancy between the goal evaluation and the measurement of program objectives is the best index as to the responsiveness of the program objectives to goal statements. In the final analysis, it is the goals which must be satisfied no matter how well the objectives are being met. If we accept the goals obtained from *Goals for School Mathematics,* we can establish an evaluation procedure which can help us to determine whether these goals are being attained. At this point we will state the goals and guidelines for evaluation in connection with our hypothetical elementary school math program.

GOAL ONE

All young people should acquire the technical skills of mathematics.

Guidelines for evaluation:
1. Determine which operation skills and measurement skills are considered to be vitally essential for the needs of society.
2. Identify those skills which are best allocated to the elementary grades in terms of mathematical priorities and the logical sequence of learning, and the psychological development of the elementary child.
3. On a paper and pencil test measure the ability of a random sampling of elementary school graduates to perform the operations and measurement skills which have been identified as important.

GOAL TWO

Skills should be interwoven into the acquisition of new concepts and not presented in isolation. (A process goal.)

Guidelines for Evaluation: (Note—since this is a process goal, evaluation must take place "in process" rather than at "end product.")
1. Describe and illustrate for teachers what is meant by interweaving skills into concepts.
2. Supervise the teaching procedure to determine whether the proper instructional process is being used.

GOAL THREE

Young people should learn the major concepts of mathematics. These concepts should be selected not because they are modern but because they have organizing power and therefore contribute to the learning structure.

Guidelines for Evaluation:

1. Determine which concepts of elementary school mathematics meet the criterion established in the goal.
2. On a paper and pencil test measure the ability of a random sampling of elementary school graduates to work with concepts to demonstrate that their functional meaning is understood.

GOAL FOUR

Creative and independent mathematical thinking should be developed by means of a discovery approach. (A process goal.)

Guidelines for Evaluation:

1. Describe and illustrate for teachers what is meant by a classroom instructional process which is conducive to a discovery approach.
2. Supervise the teaching procedure to determine whether the proper instructional process is being used.

GOAL FIVE

The concepts of mathematics and the sequence of technical skills should not be sacrificed if certain learners are slow to discover them on their own. Directed teaching should assure that these goals are attained. (A process goal.)

Guidelines for Evaluation:

1. Establish a diagnostic measure of technical skills and concept understanding. (This measure should be available in connection with performance objectives.)
2. Establish a time standard for each major learning element beyond which directed teaching will be done to assure mastery.
3. Supervise the evaluation of progress to be certain that this standard is being observed.

The goals presented here are obviously concerned with the process of instruction. This represents the best of modern thinking concerning the goals of school mathematics as postulated in *Goals for School Mathematics.* It also illustrates that it is possible to state process goals and to provide for their evaluation. When the humanizing aspects of education are considered important, it is necessary to formulate these process goals since it is tempting to ignore them if a high priority is placed on end product performance. Also *it becomes just as important to specify our process commitment as to enumerate the performance objectives.*

FORMULATING THE OBJECTIVES OF MATHEMATICS

When goals are well formulated they serve as the basis for establishing program and performance objectives. There is a major difference between product goals and process goals when we set forth to implement them, therefore we must recognize that goals two, four, and five are process goals which call for direct supervision to maintain the prescribed process. This leaves us with two product goals, one dealing with technical skills, and the other with concept development. Since goal two stipulated that the technical skills were to be interwoven with the concepts, we have a rare opportunity to combine two goals into one major goal of elementary school mathematics.

Determining the Operational Phases

In order to make a goal manageable, it is necessary to break it down into logical operations which are, in fact, major mileposts enroute to the goal. The primary purpose of identifying operations is to make analysis easier. It is not necessary that operations need to be performed sequentially even though this is most often the case. It is possible to present these operations in some other instructional order if this can be justified in terms of good learning sequence. In fact, it might in some cases be preferable to orchestrate the operations into a simultaneous teaching process. Regardless of the approach which is used, it will be necessary to identify the separate operations as the first step toward formulating program objectives.

Admittedly there are many divergent approaches which may be taken in the process of identifying the operations of elementary school mathematics. What is important is that the operations selected are functionally suited to the perceived structure of mathematics and do not interfere with commitments to process goals.

In actual practice the operations will be selected by a curriculum study committee. Often this entails adopting an established program and "buying" the operations in the process. In our case we will identify operations which seem to be compatible with the goals already formulated. These operations were selected for the following reasons:

1. Technical skills in both operations and measurement are represented.
2. Concepts are covered in the major areas of numbers, numeration, and geometry.

3. Problems are identified as a separate function which, in fact, is the application of technical skills to concept development.
4. Process goals and attitudes are viewed as general functions to be applied as an integral aspect of all operations.
5. The operations selected add up to a conceptualized structure which is both logically and psychologically sound in terms of the stated goals.

Let us assume that the curriculum study committee has completed its task. Since we need to have a set of operations in order to formulate objectives we can credit them with the following:

OPERATIONAL PHASES OF ELEMENTARY SCHOOL MATHEMATICS

I. Technical skills in operations.
II. Technical skills in measurement.
III. Concepts concerning number.
IV. Concepts concerning numeration.
V. Concepts concerning geometry.

> NOTE: Problem solving, affective outcomes, and processes identified as goals are all considered to be functions which apply to all operations as frequently as possible.

The purpose of outlining operational phases is to reveal the structure of elementary school mathematics, not to prescribe the sequence. The operational phases should satisfy Bruner's requirement that the learner acquire the power of organization which is available to him from a structure. Sequence is important only when prerequisite learning is involved.

Program Objectives for Operation I

Our performance objectives must fulfill the expectations of the goals. In the quest for means to accomplish ends, the objectives often bear little resemblance to the goals, but each objective is valid only to the extent that it accomplishes a goal. It would not be acceptable for an objective to create a new goal.

In order to illustrate the practical aspects of establishing performance objectives we will follow through with Operation I and present a set of performance objectives. There is not sufficient space to list all objectives for all operations, therefore we will resort to the procedure of selecting one section for detailed analysis through the remainder of this chapter.

This presents a good opportunity to present the essential difference between the format of a program objective and a performance objective. Operational objectives are written at the program level and although they must give some direction for performance they do not require the specific conditions or criteria for acceptable performance that performance objectives must fulfill.

ELEMENTARY SCHOOL MATHEMATICAL OPERATIONS

Program Objectives: Operation I

At the completion of elementary school each child should be able to:

A. *Addition and subtraction*
1. Demonstrate an understanding of the meaning of addition and subtraction of whole numbers, rational numbers, and integers using concrete objects or a number line.
2. Demonstrate the meaning of inverse relationship between addition and subtraction using concrete objects.
3. Demonstrate immediate recall of sums through 24.
4. Demonstrate through application an understanding of the commutative property of addition, the associative property of addition, and the identity element for addition for both whole and rational numbers.
5. Add and subtract, including regrouping of whole numbers, unlike denominators, mixed numbers, and decimals.

B. *Multiplication and Division*
1. Demonstrate an understanding of the meaning of multiplying and dividing whole numbers and rational numbers using concrete objects, regions, or a number line.
2. Demonstrate the meaning of inverse relationship between multiplication and division using concrete objects, regions, or a number line.
3. Demonstrate immediate recall of products through 100.
4. Demonstrate through application an understanding of the commutative, associative, identity elements of multiplication, and the distributive property of multiplication over division for both whole and rational numbers.
5. Demonstrate through application the property of 0 in multiplication and the reciprocal operation in multiplying rational numbers.
6. Multiply and divide whole numbers, common fractions, mixed numerals, decimals, and percentages.
7. Identify the factors of numbers up to 144.
8. Identify the greatest common factor and the least common multiple.
9. Average a set of numbers. (Provide the arithmetic mean.)
10. Solve exponential problems with powers up to 999.

We now have a complete set of program objectives for one of the five established operations. Most of the operations cited as objectives in modern mathematics texts can be classified with these 17 program objectives. Our task is not yet completed, however. It is necessary to identify the process commitments which apply to this operation

Process Commitments for Operation I

It is a departure from accepted practice to list process commitments as a separate function. In most cases they are incorporated into the objectives in some manner. In other instances they are assumed to be operational. It seems that neither of these approaches gives enough prominence to what in effect are goals entitled to the same careful consideration as the product goals. Most often these goals cannot be measured at the output state. *Detection and evaluation of process goals is best accomplished in process situations.*

Process Commitments: Operation I

1. The operations skills should be taught in a manner that makes clear the relationship between the skill and the concept involved. (Addition is basically a process of combining things and should not be initiated as a signal response to a set of numerals, for example.)
2. Wherever possible students should be able to progress at their own pace through instruction geared to their individual needs.[2]
3. Students should have the opportunity to discover some concepts and principles before didactic approaches are used. (The commutative property of addition and multiplication will be better understood and will have more power for creative and independent thinking if it is discovered rather than implanted.)
4. Directed teaching should assure that each student acquires the necessary concepts and skills if progress through discovery is unusually slow.

Performance Objectives for Operation I

ELEMENTARY SCHOOL MATH UNIT - Operation I

Performance Objectives: Addition and Subtraction - Level 10

1.1.1 a. Given a problem in addition or subtraction such as $6 + 3 = $_____ or $16 - 7 = $_____ , the student can set up the operation using concrete objects or a number line to demonstrate an understanding of the operation involved and the ability to solve the operation correctly.

1.1.2 a. Given an equation in addition with a missing addend the student can write the equivalent subtraction as in: _____ $+ 21 = 124$ to $124 - 21 = $ _____ .

1.1.2 b. Given an equation such as $23 + 24 = 57$, the student can derive $57 - 34 = 23$ and $57 - 23 = 34$.

1.1.3 a. Given any addition or subtraction with one digit numbers the student can provide the correct answer within six seconds.

---

[2] This was not listed as a goal in *Goals for School Mathematics.*

1.1.4 a. The student will demonstrate an understanding of the properties of numbers by correctly solving problems such as:

$14 + \underline{\hspace{0.8cm}} = 36 + 14$ $7 + 9 + 1 = 7 + (9 + 1)$ $21 + \underline{\hspace{0.8cm}} = 21$

$12 + 16 = 16 + \underline{\hspace{0.8cm}}$ $8 + 2 + 5 = (8 + 2) + 5$ $15 - \underline{\hspace{0.8cm}} = 0$

1.1.5 a. The student can find the sums and differences for problems in which there are not more than three numerals both with and without regrouping:

$$
\begin{array}{ccccc}
237 & 543 & 317 & 34 + 27 + 56 = \underline{\hspace{0.6cm}} & 3\_6 \\
268 & -231 & -238 & & +23\_ \\
+346 & & & & \underline{} \\
 & & & & \_78
\end{array}
$$

The following comments will help to clarify the unit performance objectives presented above.

1. The coded numbers refer back to specific program objectives outlined in the previous section.
2. Since this is the tenth unit in a sequence of thirty, not all of the program objectives are taught. (Rational numbers were not included.)
3. The sequence of skills presented is based upon Gagné's learning chain. 5 + 3 is presented before 15 + 3 for this reason. Many other sequence decisions are arbitrary and could just as easily be presented in another order. We could study all related operations simultaneously for example: 3 + 3 = 6, 3 x 2 = 6, 2 x 3 = 6, 6 ÷ 3 = 2, 6 - 3 = 3.
4. Rather than listing each specific skill to be taught, a few examples are given to illustrate the highest level of application. It is assumed that the student can perform all of the more simple operations which are not listed.
5. The criterion of acceptable performance is not repeated for each objective since this is needless repetition. The introductory statement specifies that all operations must be performed with 80% accuracy to indicate mastery and that concepts must be understood through demonstration at the 100% level.
6. The conditions of performance are not listed, again to save needless repetition. All evaluation is to take place on a paper and pencil test unless otherwise specified.
7. It is assumed that all process goals are being met through the proper method of instruction and that they will be evaluated through supervision of the instructional process.

To move from performance objectives at the level of the unit of instruction to performance objectives at the level of the daily lesson plan requires only that further specification be presented for any one unit objective. In most instances, the teacher does not wrap up an objective in a single lesson so the lesson objectives are fragments of a unit objective. We must remember that lesson objectives have no validity other than their responsiveness to the unit objectives, therefore the criterion measure of a lesson objective is relevance to the unit.

ELEMENTARY SCHOOL MATH LESSON - Performance Objectives

Operation I - Level 10 - Unit Objective I.1.1a.

1. The student will strengthen his concepts about the number twelve by combining objects which total to twelve and decomposing twelve into component parts using various manipulative objects.
2. The student will correctly record all operations as written algorithms.

All lesson objectives are means to ends procedures and must be directly related to the attainment of one or several unit objectives. In the examples given above, no criteria were established, therefore the standard of mastery will be taken as 100%. Any student who can meet both performance objectives has satisfied the requirements and need spend no further time. Nothing in this section has specified that instruction should or might be individualized but it should be noted that *performance objectives can be adapted equally well to group or individualized instruction.*

The Advantages of a Systems Analysis Approach

In finished form a systems derived course of study doesn't appear to be different from any other. Now that we have arrived at what goes on in the classroom, it looks as though teachers and students are involved in the same old familiar procedures. We can compare these two approaches in an effort to determine whether there are worthwhile advantages to systems analysis.

The most obvious advantage of the systems approach is that it is goal oriented. A good deal of effort was expended to discover what the goals of society were concerning mathematics and all lower level objectives were completely responsive to these goals. A course of study which is dedicated to goals at all levels is certainly superior to one which makes no systematic attempt to tie performance to goals.

The second advantage of the systems approach is that evaluation has been built into the program right from the beginning. Each objective states explicitly what is to happen and therefore predetermines what is to be measured. There is no apparent relationship between objectives and evaluation in other approaches.

Third, the change process is carefully calculated to take best advantage of what is good in the present setup and to involve everyone who will be affected by the change in decisions. This approach considers cost efficiency as well as morale and stands a much better change of bringing people along with the change.

Consideration of alternatives is one of the keynotes of a systems approach. At each goal and objective stage the questions asked are: "Is this the most effective way?" and, "Is this the most efficient way?" In this manner there is a constant check between objectives and performance as well as a cost analysis. Traditionally in education we find it necessary to take an all or nothing point of view. Either we use program Y or we don't. A system is much more sensitive to internal malfunctions. When something doesn't function correctly it is much easier to detect the component which is at fault. What then occurs is that we are constantly adjusting and improving the system. With traditional programs it is often impossible to detect why the results are not good, so very little modification occurs and life expectancy is limited.

Constraints to performance are examined carefully in a systems approach. With constant focus on performance and ready means to evaluate performance, the villains of constraint are unable to avoid the limelight. Whenever a problem is detected through evaluation, a search and destroy mission is initiated and the constraints are eliminated. Too often in conventional programs, there is no available means to isolate problems and amputations are performed where a pedicure would have sufficed.

The final advantage to be cited is that a systems approach is open to honest inquiry. The casual observer can compare what he sees happening with what the objectives claim is to happen. Discrepancies between performance and objectives are apparent. Ineffective or inefficient instructional methods are detected by measure rather than by hunch. Everything is laid out on the table for open investigation. When an instructional program takes on the attributes of an organic unit, it becomes sensitive and adaptable and responsive to human desires.

We have used this study of elementary school mathematics to analyze what is to be done—Operation I of a systems approach. For the second operation, design the system, we will design an individualized instruction plan which will be suitable for all basic skills areas. The final operation, operate the system, will be covered in Chapter Six where we will study a learning disabilities program in action.

FIVE

Individualizing Instruction with a Systems Approach

Operation two of a systems approach is designing the system. This chapter is intended to be a practical illustration of how a system is designed. One of the most perplexing problems that confronts educators today is determining how to individualize instruction. In order to help with this problem, we will design an individualized learning unit which can be used as a master blueprint in any subject area.

We cannot design something unless we understand the structure of what we are attempting to design. This will make it necessary to probe all aspects of the curriculum. In the end we will have a design as presented in Figures 17 and 18.

Systems design of a unit of study has a very practical application but is not a simple operation. It will be necessary to examine the organization of a course of study in technical detail in order to accomplish our purpose. For the reader who perseveres through the necessary technical details, this chapter will allow you to:

> . . . design individualized learning units.
> . . . establish management control of individualized instruction by utilizing pre-tests, individualized prescriptions, and post-tests to direct the learner through the program.
> . . . support the instructional goals of your organization by writing ad-

ministrative regulations and objectives which specify how the goals are to be accomplished.

. . . analyze the curriculum at three distinct hierarchical levels extending down to the unit of instruction, each requiring its own unique instructional process and design.

. . . design a unit of instruction by proceeding logically from putting the performance objectives in sequence to analyzing each objective in order to state the major concepts to be presented and the conceptual levels to which they are to be directed.

. . . develop a systematic procedure for analyzing the attributes of the individual learner in order to select appropriate instructional materials and learning procedures.

. . . acquire a technique for selecting the content and the presentational method of instruction in order to match individual styles of learning.

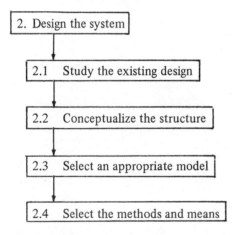

The purpose of this chapter is to illustrate how a system is designed. Although our main emphasis will be on Operation II we cannot ignore completely the first and third operations since they are essential to a treatment of individualized instruction as a system. The purpose of individualized instruction will be traced briefly from goal statements and administrative regulations to performance objectives.

In considering individualized instruction as a system, it is necessary to consider not only three distinct operations but also three hierarchical levels of organization. Figure 13 is reproduced here since it will be utilized as a map to guide this journey through an individualized instructional system.

	PURPOSE	STRUCTURE	PROCESS
Goal Level	Educational goals	Organizational structure	Process decisions
Program Level	Program objectives	Program structure	Instructional strategies
Performance Level	Performance objectives	Unit of instruction	Instructional tactics

THE PURPOSE OF INDIVIDUALIZED INSTRUCTION:
FROM GOALS TO PERFORMANCE OBJECTIVES

In Chapter Four the entire concern was to consider the purpose of elementary school mathematics. There is no intention to either duplicate or review the tasks which were outlined there, but it is necessary to establish the purpose of individualized instruction in order to give direction to designing the structure and process. The purpose will be stated in systems format since we will need to refer back to these statements throughout this chapter.

What Is Individualized Instruction?

Individualized instruction is a process which is designed to provide each individual learner with the opportunity to assess his needs, select a form of presentation suitable to his learning style, proceed at his own rate, and provide a regular source of feedback information to the learner about his performance. *Individualized instruction should offer as many options as possible to the individual learner.* Just as there is a wide variety of cognitive ability among students, there is also a large range of cognitive variety among instructional materials. There are many alternative methods of presenting instruction and each individual has his own preferred style which varies with existential conditions. Individualized instruction seeks to match each student with suitable content and an appropriate instructional process.

The Purpose of Individualized Instruction

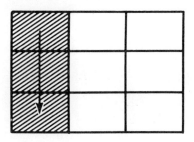

The purpose of individualized instruction should be clearly established in statements of educational goals, program objectives, performance objectives, and administrative regulations to direct their implementation. A complete set of statements will be presented in order to set the stage for designing the system.

Organizational goals. An organization justifies its responsibility to society by taking a societal goal and indicating a commitment to perform functions which will achieve the goal. In this instance the organization is the public school system and the responsible agent is the board of education.

Organization Goal 6.1 Individualized Instruction

The public schools of _____ shall promote self-realization by helping each child attain the optimum growth and development within his capacity through educational programs which take into account individual differences.

Administrative regulations. The chief administrator for the organization is responsible for developing regulations which provide information to administrators at the program level in the form of directions and restraints. Regardless of the staff levels which are consulted in this process, the final responsibility and authority rests with the superintendent of schools.

Administrative Regulation 6.1 Individualized Instruction

Each school should be organized so as to provide maximum opportunity for instruction geared to individual differences. Skills programs should be individually prescribed and study programs should contain provisions for individuals to select materials appropriate for their cognitive level and learning style.

Program objectives. Program objectives indicate how the organization is structured to accomplish its goals. Departments and courses of study are functionaries of the organization and must be responsive to organizational goals. The objectives should provide a clear indication of the expected outcomes.

Program Objective 6.1.1 Individualized Instruction

Each course of study should be so designed that individual learners can satisfy their own needs by selecting a form of presentation suitable to their own learning style. All skills programs should be individually prescribed and designed for self-management and regular evaluation of performance. Group experiences and individual experiences should be clearly delineated.

Course of study regulations. Middle managers of the organization are responsible for developing regulations which assure that organizational goals and program objectives are attained. They have the responsibility and authority to maintain the continuity of purpose at all lower levels.

Administrative Regulation 6.1.1a Individualized Instruction

All skills programs in the English department should be organized as soon as possible to provide individual diagnosis and prescription, self-management, and regular feedback of information concerning performance to both the learner and the instructor.

There can be any number of regulations to support a given program objective. The example provided was coded 6.1.1a in order that other regulations which are directed to this objective can be alphabetically coded. There would need to be a regulation concerning individualized study programs since this was not included in the above regulation.

Administrative Regulation 6.1.1b Individualized Instruction

All study programs in the English department should provide the individual learner with as many options as possible for selecting the presentational mode of instruction. Purpose should be identified with objectives rather than content so that a variety of content will be available for individual selection.

Performance objectives. Performance objectives are written beginning at the level of the unit of instruction. They are enroute objectives rather than end outcomes and provide continuity as extensions of the program objectives. There will be several performance objectives for each program objective so the example provided is only one of many.

Performance Objective 6.1.1.1ff Individualized Instruction

At the completion of this unit the student should be able to capitalize properly, when writing independently, at a 90% criterion standard.

The purpose has been indicated from goals to performance. In order to properly exhaust this topic, it would be necessary to develop a complete course outline, but the examples cited will serve the purpose of laying out the direction for the task of designing the structure and process of individualized instruction.[1]

DESIGNING THE STRUCTURE OF INDIVIDUALIZED INSTRUCTION

If there is no structure available for English 5, our task of developing an individualized program is much more difficult. Books, other media, and content do not constitute acceptable structure. *The structure of a course of study of a unit must be the conceptualized system of interrelationships which accomplish a specified objective.* It is much more efficient to treat each objective as a separate unit, or a module within each unit, since it then becomes possible to select prescribed objectives while bypassing those which are not needed. If the content field of a given textbook or filmstrip is accepted *in toto,* all of the options for selecting prescribed objectives, preferred presentational format, personal interests, and suitable conceptual level are unavailable. Individualized instruction must be designed in such a way that we can orchestrate individual routes through a field of options. Textbooks, or sections of them, and other instructional materials should be available not as ends in themselves, but as means to accomplish ends. They should be selected because their presentational form is most suitable for the individual, their conceptual level is appropriate, or because they appeal to someone's interest.

Far too frequently, specific instructional material is selected, based solely on the attribute of content. A certain film is considered to be ideal for presenting information about life in African villages. In making our decision based on content, we neutralize all of the other attributes of films in general and of this particular film. Films are usually didactic. They present a continuous stimulus; audio and visual input channels carry information simultaneously. They are representational and director biased. A particular film can be highly didactic yet overloaded with facts,

---

[1] Appendix A presents another illustration of how regulations and objectives direct classroom performance to goals of the organization.

prone to hasty generalizations, and biased in many other ways. Films, or any other media, are not suitable for universal prescriptions.

When media are selected as options available to teacher strategists, it is possible to make decisions based upon objectives. If a process goal indicates that inquiry is preferred as the route to understanding a certain principle, a filmloop would probably be more suitable than a film. Where a child is functioning at the concrete level of conceptualization, Cuisenaire rods would be far more valuable than printed equations. Many more examples could be cited to illustrate why content and media should not be permitted to be treated as structure. Where then do we look for the structure which serves as the framework within which content, media, and presentational form are options?

Organizational Structure

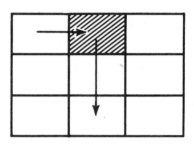

In most instances the organizational structure has been predetermined in the form of autonomous departments. We have a unit of instruction on Brazil within a South American course of study in the social studies department. It is assumed that at one time the departments were identified as the most efficient means of compartmentalizing the organizational goals. This, of course, in not true. Departments were established historically as efficient means of attaining the priority goals of a given decade. In the process, new programs of curriculum were added but seldom was the total organization reconceptualized. Each autonomous department, however necessary, must be viewed as a barrier to an organic synthesis of knowledge.

Prior to the fourteenth century, theories about the internal structure of the body were based on observation and deduction of exterior bodily functions. Avicenna's proclamations concerning the placement and function of human organs were accepted as dogma. When dissectionists finally were able to explore the internal organs, they reported only those observations which verified Avicenna and ignored completely the exciting evidence of internal networks and systems which were plainly there to be seen. In education today, we are discovering that a new synthesis of knowledge which cuts across traditional disciplines is necessary in order to deal meaningfully with ecology, biochemistry, histology, relativity physics and the other syntheses which are constantly emerging to exploit the power of combined disciplines to deal with human problems.

In the ninteenth century, 18 new specialized disciplines were introduced; psychology, archeology, biophysics, physical chemistry, etc. In the twentieth century, 11 specialized disciplines were added including, radiobiology, acyrogenetics, polymer chemistry, and radio astronomy. In the nineteenth century, 10 disciplines were created to bridge the existing disciplines; molecular biology combined cytology and genetics, and quantum mechanics joined mechanics and atomic physics. Not one of these new combined disciplines eliminated a discipline. Throughout history only one academic discipline has been eliminated and that was alchemy! There were a total of 43 academic disciplines in the eighteenth century and now there are 83 with more to come.

But who is challenging the narrow isolation of the separate disciplines and their refusal to communicate with each other? We accept them as dogma even though massive evidence indicates that knowledge has more organizational power when it cuts across the disciplines. Only the general systems theorists are speaking out and even they are catalogued and shunted to a department in the university rather than being consulted about meaningful new syntheses.

The organizational structure which we accept so willingly has tremendous influence on the structure of courses of study and units. For this reason, if we are expected to deal honestly with the structure of these subordinates, we should insist that the organizational structure be submitted to searching analysis so that a meaningful synthesis might be developed.

Many of the difficulties which are encountered at course of study and unit levels are due to the restrictions imposed by the organizational structure. It is possible to work around these limitations by creating program structures which are more related to goals than to organizational structure, but this causes internal strife since the authority hierarchy will fight to preserve its autonomy. It would be more effective if academic councils responsible to a general system or true university were more powerful than the department chairman. (In those instances where this seems to be true, the responsible leader, the dean for example, is not the effective leader.)

Program Structure

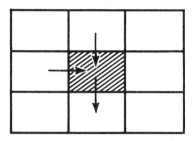

The program structure is responsive to both the organizational structure as indicated in the previous section, and to the program objectives. The problem for the designer therefore could be stated: given the program objectives to be attained and the restrictions imposed as parameters by the departmental organization, design a program structure.

The function of a program is to accomplish its purpose. If, for example, there were six program objectives, A through F, which could be presented in any order and without dependent relationships among them, they could be arranged as separate unordered functions: C-D-A-F-B-E or D-F-E-C-B-A. If it were necessary to present two or more objectives in a sequence as separate but ordered functions, this could be indicated as B→D→F-C-A-E or A-C-B→D→F-E, either of which indicate that objectives B, D, and F should be presented in sequence while order is not a concern otherwise. Where two sets of objectives are so closely related that they should not be separated into different units or modules, this relationship can be indicated: (C-D)-F-(A-B)-E where order is not a factor or (A→C)-D-(B→E)-F where order is important. It is possible, using these signals to analyze the presentational order of program objectives even when the interrelationship is quite complex: A-(F→G)→D→(B-E). The meaning of these directions should be clear at this time. The first task in designing a program structure therefore is:

1. Order the Objectives

Analyze each objective. Once the objectives have been put in order, it is necessary to analyze each objective to be certain that its intent is fully comprehended. We will examine a program objective specified for social studies in the intermediate grades to illustrate this procedure.

Program Objective 3.3.8 Intercultural Understanding

> Compare the way in which different societies meet man's common basic needs.

Why? What is it that the learner is expected to come away from this experience with? It is necessary to look at each program as a theory in order to understand what is intended. Basic to every objective is the proposition that by performing as directed the learner will attain a societal goal:

> By comparing the ways in which different societies meet man's common basic needs, the learner will understand how man's behavior is affected by physical, social, and technological factors, and will better understand human relations and his own personal transactions.

There are several propositions present in this objective when it is looked at as a theory:

1. All men have the same basic needs.
2. Societies of men meet these needs differently.
3. There must be variables within each society which cause them to develop their own solution strategies.

This analysis is essential for practical reasons. It makes apparent exactly what the objective intends for the learner. We can now proceed to identify the major concepts which must be considered; analyze the various cognitive levels which are involved; and design the structure. Note there are no specifications concerning facts or skills since they were not specified in the objective. This will permit us at performance levels to select content material based upon interest, availability, suitability, and individual need. Any skills which the learner needs in order to profit from this objective, are related to his ability to handle the instructional materials. In this case, prerequisite skills are not a factor since even the child who cannot read can meet this objective through other presentational forms. This is a question of process rather than structure and will be taken up in the next section.

It is important to note that this analysis relates specifically to the program objective given as an illustration. There will be cases when objectives deal with skills, (i.e., write a simple invitation to parents) or even specific factual content. In either case, the analysis will pinpoint the theory and the essential ingredients will be revealed in preparation for designing the structure. The second task in designing a program structure is:

> 2. Analyze each objective.

Identify the major concepts. Next in line come the major concepts. These should be identified along with several examples of second line concepts to make the relationship clear. This can be applied to the objective which is under consideration:

MAJOR CONCEPTS

Society	Common Needs	Variables	Unique Solution
City	Food	Geophysical	Hunting
Village	Clothing	Cultural	Agriculture
Nomadic Tribe	Shelter	Technological	Education
etc.	etc.	etc.	etc.

The major concepts will form the prime components of the structure. The secondary objectives are only examples from a field of alternatives which are available. Unless it is absolutely necessary to specify secondary objectives at the performance objective level, it is better to allow the learner the choice of selecting those options which are most appropriate for his needs. The third task then is:

> 3. Identify the major concepts.

Examine the cognitive levels. A common mistake is to assume that each objective has one cognitive level on a taxonomy such as Bloom's. In most instances several of the cognitive levels are involved and it is conceivable that one program objective could involve all six of Bloom's levels. A simplified taxonomy[2] will be used here to indicate how this is done.

---

[2]The RISE taxonomy is a simplified version of Blooms's categories and was devised for this book. It combines comprehension, application, and analysis under the heading "infer." In practice, the six levels are cumbersome and therefore are not used except as an academic exercise. By combining the categories which have caused the most difficulty, this RISE scale should prove to be more useful if less accurate.

COGNITIVE LEVELS

Level   I.   *REPRODUCE*. Reproduce facts, ideas, principles, in the form in which they are presented. (For program objective 3.3.8 the student should be able to recall on demand the basic needs of man and the major variables which cause him to solve these problems differently. This should only be done after there has been ample opportunity to speculate about these factors at the evaluate level.) (Level IV)

Level II.   *INFER*. Take the original knowledge and utilize it by applying it in a new situation. This level demonstrates comprehension, application, analysis, deduction, and inference. (Program objective 3.3.8—Infer from experiences why certain needs are called common needs. Discover how a given society meets its basic needs. Analyze a society to discover the factors that influence its methods of solving needs. Compare the way in which two societies solve the same need.)

Level III.   *SYNTHESIZE*. Create a new organization of ideas or procedures. Establish new relationships. (Program objective 3.3.8—Invent a new classification of variables which affect needs solutions. Form generalizations about homes of primitive peoples, food of people in cold climates, etc.)

Level IV.   *EVALUATE*. Judge the value of ideas and procedures. Make hypotheses. (Program objective 3.3.8—Evaluate the effectiveness with which two compared societies meet their needs. Before collecting data, hypothesize about major factors which influence solution strategies. Speculate about those needs which are common to all men.)

This examination of each cognitive level is necessary in order to direct the teacher to learning experiences at higher levels. It would be possible to meet the requirements of objective 3.3.8 with straight didactic teaching. If process goals have been established, such as encouraging inquiry, they must be introduced as procedures in task 3 if they are to be part of the system. This is our only opportunity to implant process into the structure. The fourth task then is:

> 4. Examine the cognitive levels.

Design the structure. All of the elements are now on hand for designing the structure. The design is only a conceptualization of the first four tasks and needs the support of task descriptions for complete understanding. Once the tasks have been completed, the model presents a graphic indication of the important interrelationships which are embodied in the program objective (Figure 16).

Figure 16
A Model of a Program Objective

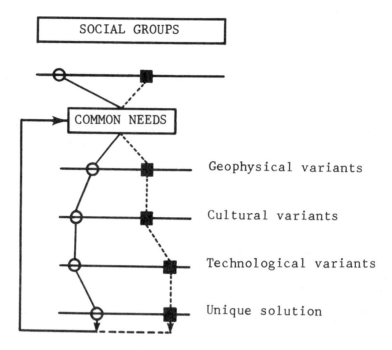

Our program objective has now been analyzed and synthesized. Consider how much easier it will now be to develop performance objectives at the unit level to support this objective. Consider also the implications for the process of instruction which now becomes an interesting function of selecting those presentational options which are most appropriate. With a structure such as this, process strategies have been left wide open and the many options which are needed for individualized instruction are available as options. *We have not been locked into specific content or instructional materials!*

The tasks which were outlined for designing a program structure can now be summarized:

1. Order the objectives.
2. Analyze each objective.
3. Identify the major concepts.

4. Examine the cognitive levels.
5. Design the structure.

Unit of Instruction

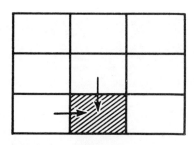

The unit of instruction descends from the program structure and should be responsive to the performance objectives. Except for the fact that it represents a lower level of instruction, it is similar in structure to the program of instruction and is designed in the same way. All of the tasks outlined above apply step-by-step to unit of instruction design. It would be redundant to follow the same procedure in detail, therefore we will utilize this section to follow a performance objective for a unit of instruction through each of the steps without bothering to repeat the rationale.

Order the objectives. We will take a set of performance objectives for a unit in numeration at the upper primary level as developed in the Elementary Mathematics Curriculum Guide of Clark County, Nevada. This particular set of objectives was chosen because it has been operational since 1968 and also since it will allow us to see how skills are dealt with using the five tasks.

Performance Objectives: Numeration - Grade Three

A. The student can identify, name, read, and write many different names for the same number. For example: $14 = 10 + 4 = 2 \times 7 = 20\text{-}6$, etc.
B. The student can identify, name, read, and write numerals for whole numbers.
C. The student can read and write number words through nine hundred ninety-nine.
D. Given a numeral such as 8073, the student can identify, name, and distinguish the numerals that are in the ones, tens, hundreds, and thousands.
E. Given a numeral, the student can name the place value for each digit.

F. Given a numeral such as 4444, the student can write the expanded numeral (4000 + 400 + 40 + 4).

G. Given a numeral such as 12, the student can write the Roman numeral XII.

H. Given a Roman numeral such as XIV, the student can write the Arabic numeral 14.

I. Given a model of three-eighths, the student can identify, name, read and write a numeral (fraction) for the rational number associated with the model.

Letters were used here in place of the numerals which were used in the source since numerals tend to suggest ordination and the thesis of this section is that ordination must be designed. It should be immediately apparent that A should come at the end of the list rather than being first since it assumes abilities which are presented in all other objectives. The reader can develop his own ordination as an exercise and then check it against the order developed here.

$$B \rightarrow C \rightarrow (E \rightarrow D) \rightarrow F \rightarrow (G \rightarrow H) \rightarrow A \rightarrow I$$

Analyze the objective. Performance objective F was selected as the focus of the next few sections. The numerals will be changed since it is difficult to use a numeral with all 4's to differentiate place value.

Performance Objective 1.1.2.5 Numeration — Upper Primary

Given a numeral such as 2468, the student can write the expanded numeral (2000 + 400 + 60 + 8).

Expressed as a theory, the above objective would be changed to indicate the rationale:

The purpose of expanded notation is to develop a more meaningful insight into the multiple aspects of a number and will provide a numeration process which will allow later operations to be meaningful rather than mechanical.

Identify the major concepts. The only concepts presented here are those embodied in this objective. There are prerequisite concepts but they are not a part of this instructional unit. The pre-test should identify such shortcomings.

NUMERAL	PLACE VALUE	EXPANDED NOTATION
Identify,	Ones	$68 = 60 + 8$
Write,	Tens	$468 = 400 + 60 + 8$
Read:	Hundreds	$2468 = 2000 + 400 + 60 + 8$
1 to 9999	Thousands	

Examine the cognitive levels. The RISE hierarchy will be used again. Even though this objective is performed at the Infer level there are essential activities to be performed at other levels:

REPRODUCE	It is recommended that all reproducing be avoided for this objective.
INFER	Given a whole number of up to four digits, identify, read, and write it. Identify place position in ones, tens, hundreds, and thousands. Given a numeral such as 2468, write the expanded notation.
SYNTHESIZE	Discover expanded notation before being shown how. Perform operations with expanded notation before being shown how.
EVALUATE	Judge with 100% accuracy the correctness of four place expanded notation performed by someone else.

Design the structure. The task here is to develop a model which conceptualizes the objective in graphic form. This is not a difficult task in mathematics.

2468 = 2 thousands + 4 hundreds + 6 tens + 8 ones
   =2000   + 400   + 60   + 8   =2468

Instructional Process as Structure

Up to this point our concern with structure has not taken individual learners or even groups of learners into account. A universal design has been prepared as a prescription for anyone who has arrived at an objective on a continuum of progress. It is assumed that the pre-test will screen out all those who are either not ready for the objective or who can already perform the function.

In the process analysis our total concern will be for the learner, either as an individual or as a member of a certain defined group. In selecting the process of instruction we are establishing a strategic match between the structured program and the individual learner. *Our first task is to consider the learner.*

Consider the learner. What are the characteristics of the group of students for whom the program is intended? If our program is to be individualized, what are the characteristics of the individual student? Since we are about to select the instructional process we need to know something about the learner for whom the content, presentational options, and media are to be selected.

The learners can be assessed by analyzing their characteristics in three major categories: sensory-motor, social-emotional, and intellectual. When we are planning for a group, we need to know the normative characteristics which describe the large majority of students. In an individualized program it is necessary to know how each individual deviates from the norm. In either case, the same considerations must be investigated.

Sensory-Motor, Receptive
1. Visual development
2. Auditory development

Sensory-Motor, Integrative
1. Visual perception
2. Auditory perception

Sensory-Motor, Expressive
1. Visual to motor (Writing and spelling)
2. Auditory to motor (Speech)
3. Body rhythm

Social-Emotional, Integration
1. Attention
2. Behavior
3. Effort
4. Interest

Intellectual, Receptive
1. Preoperative-operative-formal
2. Conceptual readiness

Intellectual, Integrative
1. Verbal intelligence
2. Performance intelligence
3. Deviant factors of intelligence

Intellectual, Learning style
1. Motivation, intrinsic or extrinsic
2. Reflective or impulsive
3. Overt or covert
4. Confident or apprehensive

Intellectual, Personal preference
1. Work with things.
2. Work with people.
3. Work with ideas.

This brief outline is only intended to be suggestive of the learner attributes and variables which must be taken into account. We will soon demonstrate that the content, presentational options, and media which are selected are directed to a certain mode of response. There are many ways to indicate understanding, but if the presentational form calls for a written response we must be aware of the normative development of the group or the ability of the individual since we are concerned primarily with understanding, rather than writing skill.

Survey the process goals. Our second task is to survey the process goals to determine if there are prescribed processes which must be considered. In Chapter Three we learned that process goals can be established even at the organization level.

1. Each learner is a unique person. Programs should be established which take individual differences into account.
2. Learning how to learn may be as important as the learning itself.

These are instructional processes which have been sanctioned at the highest level. Whenever we are designing the process of instruction we should consider the possibility of incorporating process goals in the procedure.

In Chapter Four an examination of *Goals for School Mathematics* established that three of the four major goals developed were process goals.

1. Technical skills should be interwoven into the acquisition of new concepts.
2. Creative and independent mathematical thinking should be developed by means of a discovery approach.
3. Directed teaching should be used to acquire concepts and technical skills when discovery comes too slowly.

Certainly the instructional designer would be remiss if he did not heed these injunctions. These goals are very specific concerning how instruction should take place and are direct orders to the designer which cannot be ignored. When the process is incorporated into the objectives it should be easily picked up in task 2, analyze each objective. When it is in the goal statement it is even more important, therefore we have specified that it be considered as a process task to be certain that it is not overlooked.

Select the content. Task 3 is to select the content. It is significant that this task is performed after the structure is established. Consider how much more advantageous it is to be able to select contect to meet the needs of a given group or to take advantage of other local conditions. It is preferable to set up broad parameters for content so that the individual learner can select from among several options.

Content is not media and it is not a presentational form. It is the field of data which is considered appropriate as supportive material for reaching the objective. If we consider program objective 3.3.8, which has been examined in detail in this chapter, we can see how content is selected. It has been established that we will be comparing two societies which could be tribes, villages, countries or any other social group desired. It has also been determined that we will concentrate on how these groups satisfy man's common needs, food, clothing, shelter, affection, etc. Since the variable effects of geography, culture, and technology are to be considered, the groups which we select should be different in as many of these variables as possible. We could select ten pairs of social groups based on factors such as these:

1. For which social groups is there abundant material available in various media?
2. Which social groups display the effect of a variable upon the method most dramatically?
3. Is it desirable to study new areas or reinforce areas previously studied?

When the ten pairs of societies are selected based on the criteria listed they should be presented as options. For example: From the following ten pairs of societies select the pair which will best serve your needs. (This may be directed to the class group or to an individual learner.)

An Amazon primitive village—A rural town in Switzerland
A small coastal town in Maine—A primitive Eskimo community
A village in southern Mexico—A small city in Norway,

Select the presentational options. There are many options to select among when we consider presentational form and it is helpful to consider three categories separately; representational model, message channel, and group structure. The **representational model** is the manner in which the original learning experience is re-experienced by the learner. There are three major possibilities:

Representational Model
1. *Encounter.* First hand experience with things, people, or ideas.

2. *Simulation.* An approximation of a real life experience replicated as closely as possible.
3. *Symbolic.* A sign or symbol selected to convey the essence of a thing, a person, or an idea.

Encounter with things is made possible by bringing realia into the classroom or bringing the class to the realia. Encounter with people is accomplished in the same manner. In the area of ideas problems arise. When contact with ideas is arranged, there is a temptation for the presenter to become didactic. In true encounter the idea must be open to honest inquiry. The idea may be presented from a bias, but the presenter must be non-judgmental concerning the ideas of students. Data can be incorrect and opinions can be irrational, but ethical decisions, however eccentric, can only be changed by the student himself as modified by further experience.

Simulation is a reasonable facimile of a real life experience. It attempts to replicate the original experience in as many ways as possible. A photograph, a model, or a game simulation all fall into this category.

Symbolic representation is any attempt to convey meaning through a sign or symbol. These can be applied to things, people, or ideas and range from the simplicity of a directional arrow to an intricate theory. Signs and symbols can be differentiated, but the purpose of this task would not be enhanced by this distinction.

The **message channel** is a description of the physical characteristics of the message transmission. These alternatives are familiar as auditory, visual, auditory-visual, and tactile-motor and need no comment. **Group structure** refers to the manner in which the learners are grouped for the learning experience, in a large group, seminar group, tutorial pair, or individualized.

A large instructional group is any number in excess of 14 learners. This would be the choice when the presentation is didactic and overt learner interaction is not necessary. Lectures and other media presentations of didactic nature would be involved. Large groups are seldom felt to be the preferred method for instructional purposes but are selected because it is large groups which make seminar and tutorial groups possible.

The seminar group consists of fewer than fifteen pupils. It is felt that this is a size which makes optimal involvement possible. It should be obvious that the use of seminar groups for didactic presentations is not desirable.

Tutorial pairs can be any two persons who are involved with an instructional objective together, one of whom is presumed to have already reached the objective. The tutor could be another student in the class as well as the teacher.

Individualized learning can be individualized progress in a skills continuum or any form of individual study. Individual skills would be studied when directed by a teacher prescription and individual study would be under the control of a contract with the teacher. Either individual skills or individual study can be conducted alone, in a team of two to four students, as team learning, or in a very large group. *The task of the individual, not the size of the group, determines whether or not the process is individualization.*

The presentational form, the content, and the learner's characteristics will all be considered in the process of selecting media. In our next task we will select from the alternatives in order to make the best match between the learner and the instructional medium to be used.

Selecting the media. All processes of instruction are strategies when conducted at the program level, or tactics if the level is the unit of instruction or a lesson. Within each unit there are organic modules of instruction and within each module there are learning episodes. No matter what the level, the process of media selection is the same.

It is possible to have as many as ten media choices in a sixty minute lesson. Obviously there could be thousands of media decisions in a school year. The process established here is one of establishing a pattern for decision making such that the ten decisions for a lesson involve a quick check of the best match between the learning style of a group or individual and general process strategies. Conditions of learning for this objective, process goals, content selection, presentational options, and management control requirements will all have to be considered.

There is no simple formula for selecting media. As we have seen there are many variables to consider and even a three dimensional matrix would be inadequate. The attributes of a specific medium are complex and few research studies have been devoted to attributes rather than the medium itself.[3] The procedure which seems most effective, short of a multivariate computer program, is a task order checklist. In order to demonstrate this, we will take a specific individual and a specific performance objective and come up with a recommendation concerning media.

MEDIA RECOMMENDATIONS FOR PERFORMANCE

Objective 1.1.2.6 - Numeration

---

[3] One of the few exceptions is: *Specification of Film Attributes* by Salomon and Snow in the fall, 1968 edition of AV Communication Review.

Performance Objective 1.1.2.5 Numeration — Upper Primary

Given a numeral such as 2468, the student can write the expanded numeral (2000 + 400 + 60 + 8).

Task 1   *State the conditions of learning for the objective.*

Although this objective could be satisfied at the level of a stimulus-response chain, we have established earlier in this chapter that we expect the learner to understand the principle involved. The conceptual level of the learner will determine the condition:

Level A Problem solving
Level B Problem solving
Level C Chaining

Task 2   *Consider the learner.*

We are interested here in the learner's abilities. It is more practical to list the learner's limitations which we will do, but it should be emphasized that our purpose is to identify the learner's best learning route.

FRED SMITH

General disabilities. —Fred has problems in these areas:

Auditory integration. When procedures are presented verbally to the class, Fred has difficulty understanding what he is supposed to do.

Verbal intelligence. His verbal intelligence is below average and considerably below his performance intelligence.

Factorial intelligence. Fred's vocabulary is very low.

Learning style. In response to verbal learning, Fred needs extrinsic motivation, he is impulsive in responses, he prefers overt response, is apprehensive. None of these traits are observed in performance learning. He prefers to work with things.

Specific disabilities for this objective.

Conceptual readiness. Fred is ready for this objective at Conceptual Level C.

Specific interest. Fred is interested in this objective at the concrete performance level.

Task 3   *Survey the process goals.*

There are three process goals to be considered; individualize the instruction, integrate skills and concepts, and utilize a discovery approach intitially.

Task 4   *Select the content.*

There were no alternatives presented in this case.

Task 5   *Select the presentational options.*

Representational model. The encounter level is unquestionably best.

Message channel. Tactile-motor forms are preferred.

Group structure. Individualized instruction is mandated. Tutorial instruction may be used but should not be necessary.

Task 6   *Consider management control requirements.*

Since this is to be individualized instruction, provisions should be available for routing Fred to the proper instructional step based on regular diagnosis of feedback information of progress.

Task 7   *Select the media*

It is clear that no one medium such as a textbook, programmed instruction, or a filmstrip will be suitable for Fred. The following recommendations are made:

a. Use a tutorial introduction to the performance objective.
b. Attempt to develop discovery by providing Dienes blocks and Cuisenaire rods.
c. Utilize worksheets with pictorial models and simple expanded notation.
d. Filmloops are appropriate as supplementary aids but films, texts, and tapes do not suit Fred's learning style.

It should be clear at this point that this is a strategy for mathematics learning for this individual and that it would not be necessary to reproduce the tasks for each objective. Fred's general disabilities are relatively constant and his specific disabilities would probably be the same for mathematics skills learning. These should be reviewed for exceptions however. The media selection will then be based upon the media which are available and appropriate for each specific performance objective.

Establishing the management control network. Management control is a process of comparing performance at any given time with the objective. This requires a detection process for acquiring information about achievement at a task, and an evaluation system for comparing progress with standards. Deviation correction may be automatic, as with progress tests which reroute the learner to the proper instructional episode, or they may be made by the instructor who is able to monitor progress and intervene where necessary. The management control network for performance objective 1.1.2.5 is an individualized learning unit which will now be considered.

DESIGNING INDIVIDUALIZED LEARNING UNITS

If instruction had been available as a system it would not have been necessary to spend the greater part of this chapter laying the groundwork

Figure 17
A Conceptualized Model of an Individualized Learning Unit

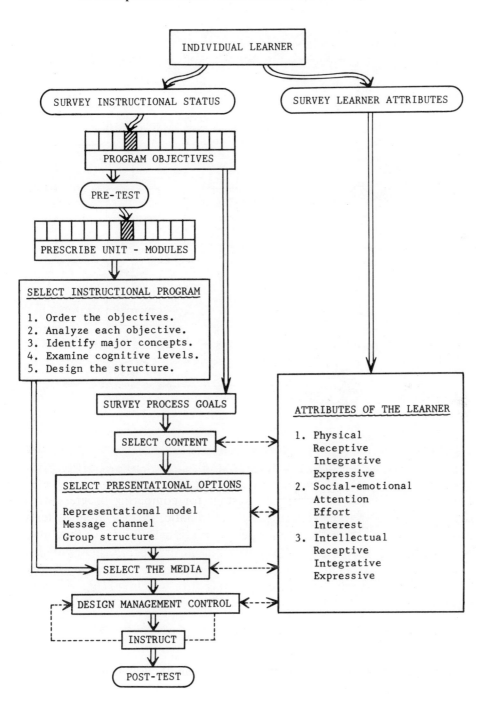

Figure 18
Management Control Flow Chart for an Individualized Learning Unit

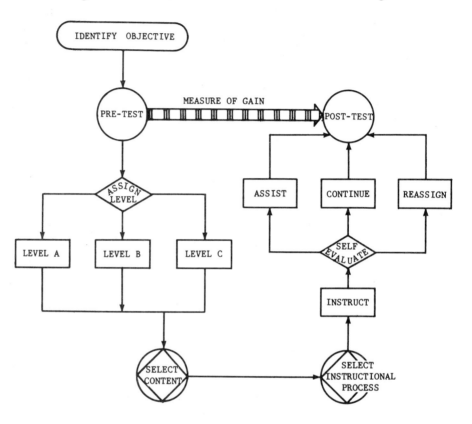

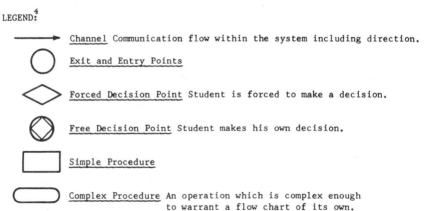

LEGEND:[4]

——→   Channel Communication flow within the system including direction.

◯   Exit and Entry Points

◇   Forced Decision Point Student is forced to make a decision.

◉   Free Decision Point Student makes his own decision.

▭   Simple Procedure

⬭   Complex Procedure An operation which is complex enough
                         to warrant a flow chart of its own.

[4] Yee, Shores, Skuldt, *Systematic Flowcharting of Educational Objectives and Processes.* (AV Communication Review, Volume 18, Number 1, Spring 1970.)

for the stated purpose which was to design an individualized learning unit. On the other hand, if we had started with this design, our result would have been a structured procedure for an unstructured process. As the individualized learning unit is developed, it should be apparent that the procedure acquires its usefulness only when instruction is viewed as objective attainment rather than a content medium.

All of the tasks which have been examined can now be combined in a conceptualized model of an individualized learning unit. (See Figures 17 and 18.)

In this chapter we were forced to consider the third operation, manage the system, because it is so essential to individualized instruction. There is still a need to consider the details of systems operation including the mechanics on the management control system. This will be accomplished in the next chapter, "Organizing a Learning Disabilities Program."

SIX

Organizing a Learning Disabilities Program: Prescriptions, Contracts, and Accountability

This chapter will illustrate how management control is applied to a learning disabilities program. The material presented will enable the school administrator:

> ... to set up a management program for identifying learning disabilities.
> ... to collect and classify test data about youngsters with learning problems.
> ... to set up a program which automatically provides a prescription for a specific learning disability.
> ... to draw up a contract of accountability.

The third and final operation of a systems approach is operate the system. In this chapter, all of the devices which have been designed to permit efficient and effective management control will be applied to a specific learning disabilities program. The learning disabilities area was selected because it is a field in which there is considerable current interest and concern. Another reason for selecting this area is that there are few management models available to influence our application. The procedures outlined here can be applied with modification to an individualized instruction unit in mathematics or a college course in anthropology.

In Chapter Five we were forced to deal at length with all three operations in order to design a complex system—individualized instruction. In this chapter, we will not need to recapitulate other operations. Operation two, design the system, will be assumed to have been completed. In other words, the many management techniques which will be used here were designed ahead of time in a design operation which will not be reviewed. The purpose of a system is explicated in operation one and although we will not examine this operation there is no neater way to set the stage for a systems application than to review the goals, objectives, and regulations which established the system.

A Learning Disabilities Program for the Public Schools of _____ :

Organizational goal 1.1

The public schools of _____ shall promote intellectual discipline by providing all children with knowledge of the traditionally accepted fundamentals, such as reading, writing, and arithmetic.

Organizational goal 6.1

The public schools of_____ shall promote self-realization by helping each child attain the optimum growth and development within his capacity through educational programs which take into account individual differences.

Program objective 6.1.1 Learning Disabilities

Each school should provide for students who have problems which interfere with their ability to learn through normal instructional procedures by correcting the problem or identifying a more favorable learning modality.

Administrative regulation 6.1.1a Learning Disabilities

In order to deal effectively with learning disabilities, each school should have an accurate, up-to-date assessment of all students who have receptive, integrative, or expressive problems which interfere with their ability to learn from instructional materials usually found in their learning environment.

Administrative regulation 6.1.1b Learning Disabilities

In order to eliminate learning disabilities, each school should institute programs which prescribe planned activities the objective of which is to eliminate specific learning disabilities.

Administrative regulation 6.1.1c Learning Disabilities

In order to eliminate the devastating effects of learning disabilities which interfere with learning through the usual presentational forms, each school should identify each student who has a specific learning disability, and should prescribe instructional processes which permit the student to bypass his disability.

The purpose of a learning disabilities program has been identified. The performance objectives occur at the level in which the individual school determines how it will meet the program goals. These objectives will be dealt with as they are needed throughout this chapter.

IDENTIFYING LEARNING DISABILITIES

In order to satisfy the objectives and regulations stated, there must be a system available for classifying learning disabilities, and a means of assessing and classifying each child. Our first task will be to set up a classification system. In Chapter Five a similar classification was developed for the section headed "Consider the learner."

Learning Disabilities Classification Plan

I. Sensory-Motor problems
  A. Receptive
    1. Visual stimulus recognition.
    2. Auditory stimulus recognition.
  B. Integrative
    1. Visual interpretation.
    2. Auditory interpretation.
  C. Expressive
    1. Visual to motor (writing and spelling).
    2. Auditory to motor (speech).
    3. Body movement.

II. Social-Emotional problems
  A. Receptive
    1. Attention to task.
  B. Integrative
    1. Effort at task.
  C. Expressive
    1. Appropriateness of behavior to task.

III. Intellectual
  A. Receptive
    1. Conceptual readiness for task.
  B. Integrative
    1. Recall.
    2. Inference.
    3. Synthesis.
    4. Evaluation.
  C. Expressive
    1. Convergent production.
    2. Creative production.

This classification system meets the essential requirements of a taxonomy. Human development is considered in the three broad areas of sensory-motor, social-emotional, and intellectual. Within each area three functions are considered: receptive, integrative, and expressive. Thus, for coding purposes, I is always sensory-motor and B is always integrative. The sub-category numeration deals with the unique attributes of each major classification and therefore the coding becomes definitive rather than classified. For both the social-emotional and intellectual areas, there is very little guidance for a classification system in the way of available models. The abbreviated form of Bloom's taxonomy which was developed for Chapter Five as RISE is used again. Refer to "Program structure" for a full explanation. The social-emotional attributes presented here are suggestive only and need a great deal of development. For the moment they will serve the purpose of rounding out a classification system which is needed as a device for managing the system.

A Management Program for Identifying Learning Disabilities

Many of the things which will be discussed here are elements of existing learning programs. What will be different about this presentation is that learning disabilities are brought under management control. As administrators, we are responsible for the objectives and regulations which are established at higher authority levels. Our major function is to reduce or eliminate the discrepancy between present status and desired objectives. When we specifically quantify what we propose to do and how well we expect it to be done, we are establishing a contract of accountability.

There is not sufficient space to deal at length with each specific learning disability, so we will take one and follow it through each task to be performed in establishing management control of systems operation. The specific disability selected is I.C.1 Sensory-Motor Expression—Visual to motor.

What is the criterion standard? How will a student perform if he has adequate visual stimulus recognition? We must describe this behavior in general terms so that we can recognize the condition at which there is no problem. This condition will be rated 0. This also establishes the objective toward which all students who have a problem are to be directed. Conditions which fall short of the objective will be rated as; 1—slight problem, 3—moderate problem, and 5—severe problem

Criterion standard for I.C.1
Given a simple visual stimulus (such as goemetric outlines or letters and

words) the student can reproduce the form accurately. (Paper and pencil or a model construct.) The student can:

1. Distinguish and reproduce likenesses and differences in letters.
2. Consistently demonstrate by written response that he can distinguish between p, b, and d.
3. Can copy simple geometric outlines.

How is the criterion standard measured? Our next task is to discover means of measuring performance against the criterion in order to rate the performance on a four point scale of 0, 1, 3, or 5. Although the attribute to be measured is an absolute condition, the measurement device must be appropriate for the student's developmental level. In the examples given above, it is assumed that the student can hold a pencil and can do some reading. These measures would not be appropriate for three-year olds. Following are a few standard measures for visual stimulus recognition:

The Purdue Perceptual-Motor Survey[1]

The Visual Achievement Forms of this test provide good information about visual to motor ability which can be rated on a four-point scale. (See Figure 19.)

Figure 19
Geometric Copy Forms from the Purdue Perceptual-Motor Survey

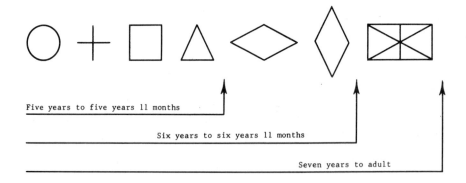

[1]Eugene Roach and Newell Kephart, *The Purdue Perceptual-Motor Survey.* (Columbus, Ohio: Charles E. Merrill Books, Inc., 1966) pp. 64-69.

In the Purdue Perceptual-Motor Survey the forms are presented on individual 4" x 5" cards. The forms are to be reproduced on a paper of sufficient size to contain all seven forms. The student is rated on both form and organization.

Rating[2]

Form

0—Adequate performance throughout.
1—Minor distortions, particularly in diamonds.
3—Any segmenting in any of the drawings.
5—"Dog ears" on diamonds, gross segmenting. Cannot produce recognizable form in one or more drawings.

Organization

0—Left-to-right, top-to-bottom, size adequate.
1—Other organization if complete. More than four of the forms are organized on the page.
3—Size is markedly too small or too large. Less than five of the forms are organized on the page.
5—No apparent organization in the drawings.

Other Perceptual-Motor Tests

There are many tests available for assessing perceptual motor ability, including:

1. A Visual-Motor Gestalt Test
Laurette Bender, New York, N. Y.: American Orthopsychiatric Association, 1938.

2. Children's Apperception Test
Leopold Bellak and Sonya Bellak, New York, N. Y.: The Psychological Corporation, 1959.

3. Frostig Developmental Test of Visual Perception
Marrianne Frostig, Chicago, Illinois: Follett, 1964.

4. Illinois Test of Psycholinguistic Abilities
S.A. Kirk, Urbana, Ill.: University of Illinois Press, 1968.

---

[2] The rating scale is revised here to conform to this chapter. The Purdue scale ranges from 4 to 1.

5. Initial Learning Assessment
Edward G. Scagliotta, San Rafael, Calif.: Academic Therapy Publications, 1970.

6. The Development Tests of Visual-Motor Integration
K.E. Berry and N.A. Buktenica, Chicago, Ill.: Follett, 1967.

Collecting the Data

When the specific learning disability has been identified, the criterion standard established, and the measurement instrument selected, it is time to set up a procedure for collecting and tabulating data. A separate form should be used for each specific learning disability and on this sheet the names of all students in a group who do not meet the criterion standard should be listed along with their rating. (Form LD-1)

Form LD-1

STATUS REPORT: SPECIFIC LEARNING DISABILITY

I.C.1 Physical-Motor Expression — Visual to Motor

Group *Room 32*   Date *4-17-70*

Evaluation *The Purdue Perceptual-Motor Survey*

The student can demonstrate that he understands what is seen by reproducing the form.

Name	Rate	Comment
Jackie Norris	3	
Kathey Jinks	5	Could not do diamond.
Frank Strom	3	Segmented last four items.

In addition to inventorying students by specific learning disability, as was done in form LD-1, it is also advisable to inventory specific learning disabilities for each student. (Form LD-2)

STATUS REPORT: *Frank Strom*   Form LD-2

| Specific Learning Disabilities Inventory |

19- **69 BR**   19-_____   19-_____

19- **70 LL**   19-_____   19-_____

19-**71 MK**   19-_____   19-_____

	11-69	2-70	4-70
I.C.1	5		5
II.A.2	1		1
II.C.1		3	

PRESCRIBING FOR LEARNING DISABILITIES

There should be available a criterion standard for each learning disabilities area which is as specific as that already proposed for I.C.1. This becomes the *terminal objective* toward which the prescription is directed. The prescription will actually consist of a number of activities directed toward sequential *enabling objectives* which are placed on a developmental continuum. In the case of I.C.1, the terminal objective calls for the ability to reproduce the seven forms in the Purdue test. A very primitive enabling objective might call for the ability to trace a circle on a form board.

It is important to note that the prescription is built on a sequence of enabling objectives, not on activities. The activities are directed to the enabling objective and may be ordered or unordered. Form LD-3 illustrates how a prescription sheet is laid out for a specific learning disability. The following information is included:

1. A record of the criterion rating at regular intervals. (Date and rating are entered at time of testing.)
2. A sequential list of enabling objectives. (The prescribed objectives are checked.)
3. The activities are numbered and coded. (Numerals not encircled represent activities to be done in sequence. Those encircled in sets can be done in any order within the set. Activities assigned are indicated by a diagonal line. Activities completed are indicated by a cross. The zig-zag line indicates the highest numeral assigned to an activity at the time.)
4. Mastery of an enroute objective is indicated by entering the date and the initials of the examiner.
5. Mastery of the terminal objective is indicated by entering the date and the initials of the evaluator. (A tutor or an aide may check an enabling objective but a *teacher* must evaluate the terminal objective.)

Form LD-3

Name *Henry Jennings*

Criterion Standard **I.C.1**

The student can demonstrate that he understands what is seen by reproducing the form.

9-69	1-70	5-70							
5	5	3							

Do	Enroute Objective	Activities	Mastery
1 __	Can hold a pencil with finger control.	A 1 2 3 4 5 6 7 8 9 B 1 2 3 4 5 6 7 8 9	1 _____
2 __	Can trace a circle and square on a formboard.	A 1 2 3 4 5 6 7 8 9 B 1 2 3 4 5 6 7 8 9	2 _____
3 **X**	Can write letters C, I, O and L following dots.	A ✗ ✗ ③④⑤⑥ 7 8 ⑨ B ①②3 4 5 6 7 8 9	3 3-70 JB
4 **X**	Can copy a circle and a square.	A ✗ ✗ ✗ 4 5 ⑥⑦⑧⑨ B 1 2 3 ④⑤ 6 7 8 9	4 _____

Terminal Objective Attained: Date 4-1-70

Evaluator **MM**

To complete the management control system for prescribing for disabilities it is necessary to have a complete set of activity cards on file for each individual student. On Form LD-3 for example there were six activities prescribed for the two enabling objectives for Henry Jennings. There should be six cards on file so that any tutor, after checking Henry's prescription on Form LD-3, could pull his card for a prescribed activity. This form is illustrated as Form LD-4.

			Form LD-4
Name **Henry Jennings**			I.C.1--3

Enroute Objective:
Can form letters C, I, O, and L using dots.
(Dot patterns and pencil.)

Activity	Date	Tutor	Comment
1	1969 11/20	JJ	O.K.
2	12/21	JJ	Not yet.
2	1970 1/5	RB	Good—O.K.
5	1/7	JJ	Trouble with L.
5	1/11	JJ	O.K. Enroute objective attained.

It should be apparent that all of the forms outlined so far are tied to objectives and are therefore not apt to change very often. Some of the prescription forms in use with individually prescribed instruction are related to activities rather than objectives. This is a procedure which will cause problems because the prescriptions will be subjected to numerous changes as effective activities become available and need to be written in. It is also not good systems procedure to allow content to dictate structure as we learned in the last chapter.

With this system, it is now possible to have activity cards on file which can be pulled for reference but which are not written upon. When an activity becomes obsolete, it is only necessary to throw away the card and assign the same coding to the improved activity (Activity Card #2).

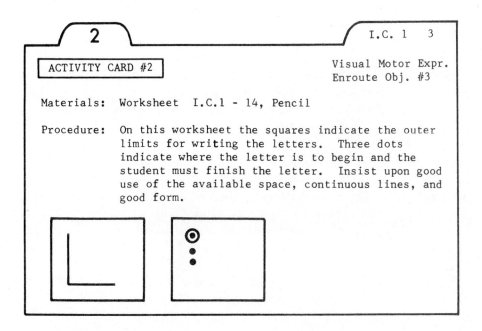

DRAWING UP A CONTRACT OF ACCOUNTABILITY

A contract of accountability is a clear-cut indication by the teacher of what he intends to do for each child. A prescription sheet is not a contract because it outlines what needs to be done but gives no indication of what will be done. A contract, on the other hand, indicates what will be done for each child in terms of objectives, cost, and time.

Contracts are drawn up between two parties to indicate the services which the first party will deliver and the method by which the service will be acknowledged by the second party. An instructional contract must have these same elements or the term is being misused. The party of the first part is the instructional representative, usually the teacher. A contract can be drawn up by a learning disabilities teacher, a classroom teacher, or any teacher of special services. The party of the second part is the representative of the person or persons who are paying for the services. Contracts are drawn up with superintendents and boards of education or with parents if they are paying for the service. The contract is the indication to the person who is supplying the funds of what will be done in return.

Contracting for changes in human behavior is certainly a new venture. It assumes that changes in behavior can be measured. It also assumes that the contractor has confidence that he can bring about the specified change within the established parameters of cost and time. As educators, we should not be caught in the perennial rationalization that ours is an inexact science which should not be held accountable to measurement. Our major concern is to keep our goal values in balance so that things which are easily measured do not receive priority because of this. We should take a page from the book of the very specialists who are held up to us as hard-nosed, practical, cost-conscious realists. Architects, physicists, engineers, and production managers are also faced with situations where things are difficult to measure, where production time is impossible to predict, or where there is even no certainty that the objective will be attained. Under these circumstances, contracts are still drawn up, money is exchanged, and accountability is the name of the game. We should see to it that accountability is not equated to mechanical assembly line type of contracting, but to the most up-to-date systems contracting that goes on in business in a technological era. We are not involved in piece work! When our counterparts in the world of business enter into contracts where there is an element of probability and uncertainty, they protect themselves by escape clauses, cost-plus provisions, and large profit margins. We would also want to avoid the unethical practices which are used to give the impression of accountability. When we find ourselves being held accountable for meeting our objectives "just as is done in business," let us be certain that we understand completely "just how it is done in business."

On a more positive note, we can approach accountability with the knowledge that there are not yet established any dire consequences for not meeting our contract. In this way it would be possible for anyone to evaluate us in terms of what we were trying to do. Included in the evaluation would be an explanation of any circumstances which interfered with objective attainment such as pupil absenteeism. Following the format established in the section on prescription, a suggested format for drawing up a contract of accountability can be offered (Figure 20).

Figure 20

CONTRACT OF ACCOUNTABILITY

Mark Johnson

Learning Disabilities Teacher, West Side School

Of the 30 students assigned to me, 85 percent will achieve a change in rating to a higher rate in at least one specific learning disability, by June 30, 1970. Students who do not receive a minimum of seventy hours of guided activity will not be counted.

Contract Satisfied? Yes   No

Student List	S.L.D.	Rtg.	6/30	Hrs.	Comment
Jennings, Henry	I.C.1	5	3		III A.2 not
	II.C.1	3	1	78	attempted
	III.A.2	1	1		this year.
Brown, Larry	II.C.1	3	3	76	
Carey, Helen	I.A.1	5	3		
	II.C.1	5	5	58	
Philips, Joe	II.A.1	3	3		Less than
	II.B.1	5	5	64	70 hours.

A. Students with 70 hours or more of treatment 26

B. Students who increased one rating or more 23

C. B ÷ A 88%

Contract terms met?   Yes <u>X</u>

No ___

SEVEN

Using Program Budgets
for Project Planning

Program budgets are for planning, not for accounting. This chapter on program budgets will help you to:

   . . . understand the distinction between program budgets and traditional budgets and state six ways in which they are different.

   . . . learn how program budgets make it possible to compare the cost efficiency of alternative ways of accomplishing a given objective.

   . . . estimate the true cost of instituting a new program including its long range implications.

   . . . measure the cost efficiency in terms of dollars per unit of output.

   . . . set up your own program budget with a five year projection which includes adjustments for inflation, enrollment increases, and capitalization costs.

A program budget is a management tool designed to integrate cost analysis with operational planning. While a traditional line item budget is concerned with where money is put into the system, a program budget is interested in the cost of the various outputs of the system. Program budgeting is utilized by educational planners rather than accountants or business managers. It is a decision making tool.

In this chapter, we will analyze a program budget in detail and contrast it with a traditional budget. Consideration will be given to its usefulness for planning, and various techniques for setting up alternative proposals for cost analysis will be examined. We will review all of the ways in which schools are applying program budgeting to solve planning problems. Finally, we will actually set up a program budget and show how it operates.

ANALYZING A PROGRAM BUDGET

Program budgets are often referred to as Planning Programming Budgeting Systems, or PPBS. This is a very appropriate title since it names the three major operations which occur:

Planning –   Alternative ways of solving a problem are compared in terms of input cost and output benefits.

Programming –   All of the activities related to achieving an objective are brought together as a program for planning and budgeting purposes.

Budgeting –   Available resources are matched with program priorities.

Traditional line item budgets are not concerned with output. All that they are expected to accomplish is to classify the money input to the system by organizational categories. The typical school budget is composed of general control, instruction, maintenance of plant, operation of plant, fixed charges, auxiliary agencies, and capital outlay. Let us consider some of the shortcomings of this type of budget:

1. Traditional line item budgets are projected for only one year. The common procedure is to adjust each category by a percentage change to correspond to the cost of living index. This tends to perpetuate whatever rationale, if any, established the initial priority of allotments. It also assumes that there is a direct relationship between cost of living changes and educational costs.
2. Line item budgets establish constraints to programming rather than assisting in program development. To introduce a new program, one must first find out what is available in the budget and then develop a program, hampered by both the limitations and excesses which are available.
3. The cost analysis data which is available from traditional budgets is mostly misleading and useless. Per pupil cost figures which appear to have something to do with accountability are usually meaningless. Per pupil cost to accomplish what? Compared to what?
4. Line item budgets do not hold financial boards accountable for their budget cuts. A reduction in a per pupil formula or a percentage cut have the effect of directing educators to do what they hoped to do, with less money. Cuts are made in input without regard to the effect on output.
5. Traditional budgets do not reflect the true cost of proposed projects. At best

they indicate the down payment cost while ignoring the number of years the program will operate.

6. The program manager or decision maker is bogged down with detail in traditional budget accounting. He is occupied in a time consuming process of classifying cost data in a format that is of very little help in planning.

Defining Planning-Programming-Budgeting Systems

Program budgeting is a management tool which is useful in a systems approach. It is not a systems approach but is often mistaken for one because it depends upon the support of data which must be made available from systems analysis procedures. If a systems approach is in operation, a program budget can be easily recognized as a series of tasks related to cost analysis and operational planning. When a systems approach is not available, this same data must be generated and the whole process is misnamed program budgeting. The relationship between a systems approach and program budgeting can be clearly seen in Figure 21.

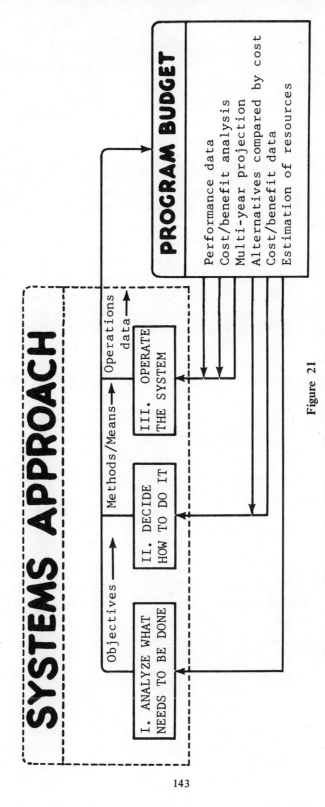

Figure 21

Program Budgeting as a Management Tool to Assist a Systems Approach

Note that the function of the program budget is to feed information to the various operations of the systems approach. The determination of what needs to be done is accomplished as an operation of the system and not by any aspect of program budgeting. When program budgeting is concerned with purpose or objectives, it only accepts the information that comes from systems analysis; it does not generate this information.

Unlike traditional budgets which classify and allocate money coming into the system, program budgeting is interested in determining the cost of the various outputs such as programs and projects. *The major function of program budgeting is to consider the feasibility of various alternatives for accomplishing objectives based on cost benefit analysis.*

PPBS brings together planning and budgeting in such a way that information about cost alternatives influences planning and information about planning determines budgeting. There are far too many situations in existence where the structure of the budget dictates what programs operate and even how they must operate. Program budgeting makes it possible for new projects to break into the organization and then to demonstrate their worth.

Let us look at traditional budgets and program budgets side by side to discover the essential ways in which they differ:

TRADITIONAL BUDGET	PROGRAM BUDGET
1. A procedure for matching resources and organizational allotments.	1. A procedure for matching resources and desired objectives.
2. An annual accounting.	2. A long range plan.
3. Who gets what?	3. What gets done?
4. Budget change decisions are based on percentage increments.	4. Budget change decisions are based on anticipated output.
5. Budgets are interpreted as limitations on spending.	5. Budgets are interpreted as current priorities.
6. Investments are allocated as payoffs.	6. Investments are related to payback.
7. The total budget is a summation of incremental changes.	7. The total budget is the best match between available resources and needs.
8. Allotments serve as constraints to decision making.	8. Allotments are determined by decision making.
9. A comptroller's budget.	9. A manager's budget.

What Are the Characteristics of a Good Program Budget?

The advantages of a program budget are implied in the comparison with a traditional budget. A program budget is a rational ordering of resource allocations based on attaining objectives, therefore this rationale can be stated directly:

1. PPBS makes it possible to compare alternative ways of accomplishing a given objective.
2. PPBS makes it possible to project the true cost of instituting a new project.
3. The long term cost of a given project is also available for scrutiny in a program budget.
4. PPBS provides a measurement of cost efficiency.
5. Expenditures which are related to a given objective can be brought together no matter how widely dispersed they have been allocated.
6. A program budget collects and organizes data with the decision-maker in mind.
7. The cost/benefit comparison of competing programs is available in PPBS.
8. Program budgets clearly indicate who is responsible for managing each activity.

The Structure of a Program Budget

A traditional budget has been criticized because it allocates money to organizational departments rather than to a project identified as the sum of all activities related to a goal. This can be seen in a typical school budget.

TRADITIONAL BUDGET

General Control
    School Board business office and supervision
    Supplies and miscellaneous office expenses

Instruction
    Salaries of teachers and principals
    Textbooks
    Stationery and supplies
    Curriculum program
    Clerical assistance
    Testing program
    Education of exceptional children

Operation of Plant
    Wages of janitors
    Fuel
    Water, light, telephone and sewers

Maintenance of Plant
   Repair of buildings
   Repair and replacement of equipment
Auxiliary Agencies
   School libraries — visual education
   Promotion of health
   Transportation
Fixed Charges
   Insurance — rent
Capital Outlays
   Equipment of buildings
   Alteration of buildings

A traditional budget serves a useful purpose and will not be replaced by a program budget. School systems which use program budgeting continue to transfer expenditures to a line item budget because it does spread out expenditures into categories which are seen as separate and which are understood by financial boards and the public. The function of the program budget is to provide the manager of the system with a decision making tool, not to replace traditional budgets. The wise manager will find that program budgets make sense to board members and to the public and therefore will use them in selling his budgets.

Classification by Programs and Projects

There is an important difference between programs and projects and an understanding of this difference is crucial. *The key to understanding the rationale of program budgets is to perceive that the ideal program budget would be composed entirely of projects.*[1] Any classification by program is a compromise with tradition. This tradition is so strong that all program budgets known to be in operation at this time have retained a program outline.

A *project* is a new activity related to attaining a specified goal. In a pure project approach all other costs, such as salaries and fixed charges, would be prorated and assigned to the project as a shared cost.

A *program* is a classification of continuing activities which are long range and which have become conceptualized by tradition as belonging together. Instruction is a program classification and would not be meaningful in a pure project approach.

The usual practice at this time is to retain a program structure at the

---

[1] It is unfortunate that the title "program budget" has become accepted since it is a "project budget" that is intended.

higher levels of the structural hierarchy while introducing projects as lower level classifications as they occur. An outdoor education project would be classified as *Outdoor Education* in this approach and *all* costs related to this project would appear here including a prorata share of supervisory costs and other supplementary services which apply.

The combined approach can be illustrated by the following classification where Instruction is extracted as one of three major areas at level I of the budget hierarchy. Only instruction will be followed through to lower levels.

PROGRAM BUDGET: CLASSIFICATION BY FUNCTIONS

LEVEL   I.   *INSTRUCTION*
                COORDINATING PROGRAMS
                BUSINESS PROGRAMS

LEVEL   II.   (Under Instruction)
                Regular
                Special
                Continuing

LEVEL   III.   (Under Regular)
                Early Childhood
                Elementary
                Secondary
                Vocational

LEVEL   IV.   (Under Elementary)
                Reading
                Social Studies
                Mathematics
                Language Arts
                Science, etc.
                Outdoor Education[2]

LEVEL   V.   (Under Science)
                In-class instruction – Primary unit
                In-class instruction – Intermediate unit
                Nature Center Field Trips[2]

The NEA Committee on Educational Finance has developed a suggested classification system which is much more objectively oriented than any

---

[2] Two projects have been introduced into this hierarchy. Each category is mutually exclusive so no outdoor education costs should be charged to science and no nature study field trips should be charged to in-class instruction.

presently in use.[3] This committee considered the program outputs of the schools and developed an outline oriented to the major goals of education. With program headings such as these, projects can be classified accurately as to purpose. The NEA Committee's outline has been modified to follow the format established in this chapter. Health has been carried to Level II and Learning has been completely developed.

PROGRAM BUDGET: CLASSIFICATION BY PURPOSE

LEVEL   I.   *PERSONAL SAFETY*
               HEALTH
               LEARNING
               SATISFACTORY HOME AND COMMUNITY ENVIRONMENT
               ECONOMIC SATISFACTION
               SATISFACTORY LEISURE TIME OPPORTUNITIES
               TRANSPORTATION, COMMUNICATION, LOCATION

LEVEL   II.   (Under Health)
               Control of infectious and contagious disease
               School nursing
               Health screening programs
               School treatment programs
               (Under Learning)
               Basic Skills
               Moral and social skills
               Individual fulfillment skills

LEVEL III.   (Under Basic skills)
               Physical self-care skills
               Independent living skills
               Specific employment skills

LEVEL IV.   (Under Independent living skills)
               Language arts
               Computational
               Reasoning

It is obvious that the choice of program budget structural format presents a dilemma. The NEA committee's outline is true to the rationale of relating costs to output objectives, but it presents problems when attempting to classify projects. One would be forced to make a very arbitrary choice in classifying outdoor education properly since at almost

---

[3] State-Local Finances Project, the George Washington University, *Planning for Educational Development in a Planning, Programming, Budgeting System* (NEA Washington, D.C. 1968)

every level there would be several alternatives. The basic problem in classifying by output objectives is that *most school activities satisfy several output objectives.* The dilemma is built into the system.

Another problem occurs when classifying according to program activities. There are many projects, such as outdoor education, that do not fall neatly into a subject category. Any project which is directed toward a unified approach to curriculum will present a problem (ecology, the humanities, etc.).

There is no easy way around this dilemma. There are many alternative approaches to developing major class headings and each of them can be mutually exclusive only at Level I. At all lower levels subclassifications must be made on an arbitrary basis. In the examples provided, we have seen classification systems based on organization, functions, and purpose. In addition, it is possible to classify by resources, by clients served, and by several other points of view. *The classification system recommended here is major classification by function with projects classified as high on the level scale as possible.* The combined approach used in the second of the three procedures described illustrates this preferred method.

Developing a Program Classification

If the recommendation is followed that major classifications should be established based on functions, each school district will want to consider the functions which are relevant to local conditions. The following guidelines are offered to assist in setting up program classifications:

1. The system used must be capable of being transferred to whatever line item budget formats that are used locally.
2. The system used must be valid for all the school districts which are encompassed in the plan.
3. The classification system must give top priority to the planning needs of program managers.
4. New projects should be kept as units rather than being dispersed into other budget categories.

Pitfalls of Program Budgetings

Program budgets are neutral management tools but as soon as they are used the biases of the manager come into play. Program budgets do not make decisions; they bring data to the manager to assist him in making decisions. Most of the limitations which will be pointed out here are the result of human fallibility. Whether a school administrator is using a program budget himself or interpreting data from someone else's work, he should be aware of these pitfalls.

1. *Schools are open systems.* In Chapter Two, it was pointed out that while closed systems respond perfectly to self-regulation and predictability, open systems are constantly subjected to outside contingency factors, such as changes in priority, which make precise control impossible. Program budgets are subject to the effect of the changes in input and output which are inevitable in an open system.

2. *Mystification can obscure specification.* There is a certain mystique involved when new sophisticated methods are used. There is a danger that those who use program budgeting will take advantage of the awe in which they are held in order to mystify others into going along with programs.

3. *The value of a program budget is measured in the quality of the decisions rendered, not the elegance of the data presented.* A poor choice of alternatives to be tested can render the process meaningless before it is begun.

4. *Elegant quantification is no substitute for relevant qualification.* No matter how sophisticated the procedure may be it is only as good as the human judgments made in deciding what to ask the system to do.

5. *What is validated can be misinterpreted as what is valuable.* When an objective can be validated, it becomes easier to sell it to the client. Often there are valuable objectives which are difficult to validate using a given procedure. Valuable objectives should not be sacrificed because they don't show up well in cost/benefit analysis. The relationship between costs and benefits is a value judgment in the final analysis.

PRESENTING ALTERNATIVE PROPOSALS

Program budgets are ideally suited to performing the function of presenting several alternative proposals for consideration. It is possible to apply cost/benefit analysis to alternative plans for accomplishing the objectives of a given project. In fact, it is highly recommended that school systems which are contemplating using program budgeting become familiar with the procedure by working out the alternatives to a project.

A case study will be presented to illustrate how cost/benefit analysis can be applied to a familiar school problem, attempting to obtain assistance for the school principal in order to increase his time available for instructional supervision.

Increasing the Principal's Supervision Time – Alternative Proposals

The program under consideration is how to increase the amount of time which the school principal can devote to supervision of instruction, direct or indirect. After a discussion involving all of the principals in town, the following procedure was agreed upon:

1. Determine by survey how much time principals now spend on instructional and non-instructional duties.
2. Consider alternative means of increasing this time.
3. Consider the effect of each alternative on the time allocation.
4. Determine the cost/benefit of each alternative.
5. List any additional benefits of each proposal.
6. Make a decision.
7. Write a proposal.

Time Allocation Survey

The time allocation survey was based on time logs kept by the principals for three months. There were twenty principals involved and the time devoted to each of four categories was averaged after eliminating the four low estimates and the four high estimates of total instructional time (%) for statistical purposes.

Table I	Analysis of present allocation of principal's time to instructional and non-instructional duties by percent.	
	Office Duties	45%
	Other Non-Instructional Duties	19%
	Total Non-Instructional	64%
	Direct Instructional Involvement	17%
	Indirect Instructional Involvement	19%
	Total Instructional	36%

Alternative Solutions

The possible means of increasing instructional supervision time were considered in two meetings devoted to brainstorming. The following proposals resulted:

A. Schedule 50% of each day for instructional time. Don't let anything interfere with the schedule.
B. Hire ten assistant principals and assign each to half time duty in the twenty schools.
C. Hire a full time clerk for each school.
D. Hire a full time assistant principal for each school.
E. Hire a full time assistant principal and a full time clerk for each school.

Effect of Alternatives on Time Allocations

This was the most time consuming aspect of the entire study. It was necessary to predict the effect that each alternative would have on the time allocation. Each principal kept a log for one month and at the end of each day checked those activities which might have been fully assumed by each of the alternatives, B through E. Each principal also considered what the effect of alternative A would have been. The following table summarizes this survey:

Table II Effect of alternative proposals on allocation of principal's time to instructional and non-instructional duties.					
	*	E	D	C	B
Office Duties	45	15	25	20	35
Other non-instructional duties	19	9	10	15	14
Total Instructional Duties	64	24	35	35	49
Direct instructional involvement	17	67	54	50	37
Indirect instructional involvement	19	9	11	15	14
Total instructional	36	76	65	65	51
* Present situation					

In the process of keeping these logs, alternative A was considered to be impractical and was dropped.

Cost/Benefit Analysis of Alternatives

It was necessary to determine the criterion measures to be used in comparing the alternatives. The following measures were agreed upon; total additional cost, five-year cost projection, increase in the number of instructional involvement days per principal per year, and dollar cost per instructional day gained.

Total cost was calculated on estimated average salary for each position times the total number of personnel involved.

B. 10 assistant principals @ $14,000	$140,000
C. 20 clerks @ $3200	64,000
D. 20 assistant principals @ $14,000	280,000
E. Combine C and D	344,000

The total instructional involvement days per principal per year was arrived at by applying the total instructional percentage for each alternative to the 180 instructional days per year. Cost/benefit could then be figured by dividing the total number of instructional days *gained* into the cost per school. (Total cost ÷ 20.)

Table III. Cost/benefit analysis and multi-year projection of alternative proposals.

Alt.	Total Cost Town-wide	Total Cost per School	Inst. Days per Year	Inst. Days Gained	Cost per Inst. Day Gained
*	—	—	65	—	—
E	$344,000	17,200	137	72	$239
D	280,000	14,000	117	52	269
C	64,000	3,200	117	52	61
B	140,000	7,000	92	27	259

Alt.	CY	Y1	Y2	Y3	Y4	Y5
E	$344,000	$357,800	$372,000	$387,000	$402,400	$418,500
D	280,000	291,000	302,500	313,600	327,600	341,600
C	64,000	66,600	69,200	71,600	74,800	78,000
B	140,000	145,000	151,200	156,800	163,800	170,800

We will trace alternative B through each step to clarify how the measures were determined. The total cost of B town-wide for the current year was established as 10 assistant principals @ $14,000 = $140,000. This cost was projected for five years (Y5) with inflation figured at a compound inflation rate of 4%. The cost per school per year is the total cost ÷ 20. Alternative B resulted in a 51% instructional involvement. (51% of 180 = 92. 92 − 65 = 27 instructional days gained.)

The cost per instructional day gained for alternative B was determined as 7,000 ÷ 27 = $259. Plan C offers the lowest total cost, the lowest per day gained, and the second best gain in instructional days at 52. It is clearly the best alternative based on the data gathered in the survey.

A final aspect of the study was to consider the benefits from each plan not specifically related to increasing instructional involvement time. Since the cost/benefit was so decisive in favor of alternative C, these supplementary benefits were not considered further.[4]

Presenting Alternative Proprosals for Consideration

There are several things which the school administrator might do with the results of the analysis of alternatives. First, he could present the study in complete form to his superiors so that they could consider all alternatives. He could also look upon the study as his personal decision-making tool and merely pass along his recommendation. A third possibility would be to make a recommendation when the cost/benefit decision is clear-cut, and to present alternatives when all alternatives are educationally feasible and additional cost clearly buys additional services.

---

[4] Obviously there are many advantages that a full time assistant principal would provide that are not assessed here. Since they are not directly related to the objective stated, and since cost factor is so decisive, they were not considered.

SETTING UP A PROGRAM BUDGET

In spite of all of the interest in program budgeting, very few school systems are actually utilizing them. The problem is that books and journals spend a great deal of time extolling the virtues of program budgeting but do not show how they are set up. There are examples available from the federal government but they are not readily adaptable to school system use. The key to a good program budget is a potent conceptualization and this is obviously something that educators will have to do. We have already considered some approaches to setting up a program classification system. Now we can use a classification by functions approach to set up a program budget.

The hypothetical budget which will be set up is for a small early childhood center housed in a separate four room building. There are three teachers for 66 children. This budget is greatly simplified in order to make it easier to follow the transactions. For the purpose of this exercise, two programs and one project should suffice to illustrate the fundamental principles of setting up a program budget.

First, it is necessary to go to the traditional budget presently in use and check off every budget item which contained expenditures related to the early childhood center. Since it is desirable to show true costs, some expenditures will be prorated and charged off to the center. These are indicated by a "%" sign. All charges which can be transferred in total are checked "x."

Task #1   Transfer budget items from traditional line item budget to the adopted program budget format. Include prorata assessments.

Rationale: Expenditures should be related to functions rather than departments. The true cost of operating each function is needed for planning purposes. All costs which are hidden in other accounts must be located and transferred. (This does not apply to overhead expenses which should be kept separate, but does include a prorata share of the salaries of administrative and special service personnel who service this function; and all capital outlay purchased for or shared by this function.)

| Early Childhood Center | | | Worksheet 1-1 |

Traditional Line Item Budget

100 ADMINISTRATION

| 0012 Salaries, Assistant Supt. | % | 600 |
| 0121 Supplies, Administration | % | 100 |

200 INSTRUCTION

| 0213 Salaries, Teachers | x | 30,600 |
| 0222 Teaching supplies | x | 600 |

1200 CAPITAL OUTLAY

1243 Equipment, Instr.	x	600
1244 Equipment, Non-Instr.	x	250
		32,750

| Early Childhood Center | | | Worksheet 1-2 |

Transfer	$	To: Function	Code
0112	600	**COORDINATING PROGRAMS**	102
0121	100	**COORDINATING PROGRAMS**	121
0213	30,600	**INSTRUCTION**	203
0222	600	**INSTRUCTION**	212
1243	600	**BUSINESS PROGRAMS**	1203
1244	250	**BUSINESS PROGRAMS**	1204

Task #2 Transfer budget items from program budget to projects which have a unique function.

Rationale: Since the purpose of a program budget is to analyze the effect of separate functions, any projects which have a unique function should be set up as a separate category. Transfer and prorate costs to this budget item. (In our early childhood budget we will set up a separate accounting for Project Outdoors. For one week the children and the staff go to an outdoor center. All related costs will be transferred.)

Early Childhood Center Worksheet 2-1	TRANSFER	Program/Project Base
100 COORDINATING PROGRAMS S $600 NS 100 CO – T 700		**100 COORDINATING PROGRAMS** S $600 NS 100 CO – T 700
200 INSTRUCTION S 30,600 NS 600 CO 600 T 31,800	$600 200 100 900	**200 INSTRUCTION** S 30,000 NS 400 CO 500 30,900
1200 BUSINESS PROGRAMS S – NS – CO 250 T 250		**1200 BUSINESS PROGRAMS** S – NS – CO 250 T 250
Code: S – Salaries NS– Non-salary CO– Capital Outlay T– Total $32,750		**400 PROJECT OUTDOORS** S 600 NS 200 CO 100 T 900 $32,750

The program/project base is the foundation upon which the program budget is built. Working from this base we will calculate the cost per output unit. We will also project the budget for five years. In order to do this, it will be necessary to figure separately the effect of cost inflation, enrollment change, and capital improvements.

Task #3 Calculate the cost per output unit for each program and project and for each sub-item desired.

Rationale: For planning purposes, it is helpful to know what each program and project costs per unit of output. Since there are 66 children in this program, our unit of output will be figured as cost per child. (We will project the cost per child for all items including the S, NS, CO, and T figures.)

Early Childhood Center Worksheet 3-1	COST PER UNIT OF OUTPUT
100 COORDINATING PROGRAMS	Salaries 472.18/
S 9.09/	Non-Sal. 10.59/
NS 1.51/	Cap. Out. 12.86/
TOTAL 10.60/	TOTAL $495.63
200 INSTRUCTION	
S 454.00/	Unit of output =
NS 6.06/	$ per child
CO 7.57/	
TOTAL 467.63/	
1200 BUSINESS PROGRAMS	
CO 3.78/	
TOTAL 3.78/	
400 PROJECT OUTDOORS	
S 9.09/ (x40)	
NS 3.02/ (x40)	
CO 1.51/ (x40)	
TOTAL 13.62/ (x40)	
CUMULATIVE	
TOTAL $495.63/	

The cost per unit of output is a potent item since it relates cost directly to function. Again it must be emphasized that the figures alone are not meaningful. They must be related to the manager's knowledge of what is going on in the system. The mere fact that a cost per unit of output is high can be explained in many ways. It is when this figure cannot be explained or is surprising that the program budget serves one of its functions. In the case under study, the cost per unit of instruction for the early childhood center can be compared to the per unit costs of other instructional programs in the school system. It can also be compared to the cost of early childhood centers in other towns. Salaries represent the major portion of these costs and in many instances are beyond the control of the manager because of a difference in salary schedules or the tenure of teachers. In these cases, the cost per unit of output for non-salary items and capital outlay will be useful.

Note that it is necessary to convert the outdoor education project to equivalent units by multiplying it by 40. This is because the project ran for only one of a total of 40 weeks. The true per unit cost is $13.62 x 40, or $544.80. This figure is considerably higher than the other cost and invites investigation.

Task #4   Calculate the effect of cost inflation over five years.

Rationale: The cost of instituting a program is not a true indication of what it will cost over the years. Inflation will effect some items consistently while others are not affected. This must be seen as projected in time.

The cost of inflation is calculated by using a compound cost of inflation based on experience. If the cost of salaries has been increasing at a rate of 4 percent per year for the past ten years it will probably continue to do so. Actually, there are formulas for predicting the effect of inflation but they are beyond the scope of this book. We will simply assume that for those costs which are affected by inflation the increase will be 4 percent per year. Even though we are only interested in total costs, it is necessary to use the S, NS, CO breakdown because: the cost of inflation is not necessarily applied in all instances, does not apply to capital outlay, and usually is compounded at a different rate for salaries and non-salary items.

Early Childhood Center Worksheet 4-1	P/P Base + 1				
	CY	Y1	Y2	Y3	Y4	Y5

	CY	Y1	Y2	Y3	Y4	Y5
100						
S	600	630	660	700	730	770
NS	100	110	120	130	140	160
CO	—	— —	— —	— —	— —	— —
T	700	740	780	830	870	930
200						
S	30,000	31,500	33,980	35,720	37,560	39,440
NS	400	440	480	520	560	640
CO	500	500	500	500	500	500
T	30,900	32,440	34,960	36,740	38,620	40,580
1200						
CO	250	250	250	250	250	250
400						
S	600	630	660	700	730	770
NS	200	220	240	260	280	320
CO	100	110	120	130	140	160
T	900	960	1,020	1,090	1,150	1,250
CUM	32,750	34,390	36,010	38,910	40,890	43,010

Task #5   Calculate the effect of enrollment change over five years.

Rationale: As enrollment changes, there may come a point where an increase in staff is necessary. The effect of this staff increase on projected costs will have to be calculated after the inflation cost is projected. Expenditures for non-salary items will also be affected by enrollment changes.

Early Childhood Center Worksheet 5-1   P/P BASE + I + E

	CY	Y1	Y2	Y3	Y4	Y5
100						
T	700	740	780	830	870	930
200						
S	30,000	31,500	44,000	45,500	48,600	52,000
NS	400	440	640	690	750	850
CO	500	500	500	500	500	500
T	30,900	32,440	45,140	46,690	49,850	53,350
1200						
T	250	250	250	250	250	250
400						
S	600	630	880	930	980	1,030
NS	200	220	320	350	380	430
CO	100	110	120	130	140	160
T	900	960	1,320	1,410	1,500	1,620
CUM	32,750	34,390	47,490	49,270	52,470	56,150

The change which occurred on worksheet 5-1 showed up in year two beyond the current year (Y2). At this point, enrollment projections indicated that an additional teacher would be needed. Up to Y2, worksheet 4-1 and 6-1 were the same. The additional salary was added in and the prorata share assessed to outdoor education was figured. With the addition of another teaching unit, the non-instructional expenditures were also increased proportionally.

Task #6 Calculate the effect of capital improvements over five years.

Rationale: The final influence on projections is the effect of capital improvements. Whatever schedule is in effect for projecting the cost of capital improvements must be reflected in the final budget.

All of the effects of the capital improvement must be calculated. For the year in which the capital improvement is anticipated each budget item should be checked to be certain that the effect on staff size, salaries, and operational costs has been considered. In the case of the early childhood center, the improvement was planned for year four and consisted of a major expenditure for creating an outdoor play area on the school grounds. It was determined that the financing costs would be $1,500 for Y4 and $1,200 for Y5. Worksheet 6-1 has been abbreviated to show only the items where the change occurred. Note that the title of the worksheet indicates P/P Base + I + E + C. This informs the analyst that inflation, enrollment, and capitalization have all been included.

Early Childhood Center Worksheet 6-1		P/P BASE + I + # + C				
	Cy	Y1	Y2	Y3	Y4	Y5
1200 CO FC	250	250	250	250	250 1,500	250 1,200
T	250	250	250	250	1,750	1,450
CUM	32,750	34,390	47,490	49,270	53,970	57,350

The estimates of expenditures related to output functions has been completed. It is now possible to apply a cost per unit of output to any set of figures on any worksheet. It depends entirely on what decisions are to be made. Remember that the unit is dollars per child so the actual projected enrollment for the year in question will have to be used. As was pointed out, these figures were used for worksheet 5-1 to predict staff changes. The projected enrollment figures were: CY–66, Y1–68, Y2–78, Y3–80, Y4–80, Y5–85.

Financial Feasibility

An important part of planning in **PPBS** is to plan the financial feasibility of the projected programs and projects over the five year period. There are various formulas for predicting future revenue based on changes in income from real estate taxation and other sources of funding. There is such a wide difference in the nature of financial resources from state to state that it is not practicable to project financial feasibility. On the basis of the analysis presented for projecting expenditures, it should be possible for school administrators to apply local formulas to produce a five year projection of anticipated revenue.

DEVELOPING TRADE–OFF PROPOSALS WITH PROGRAM BUDGETING

In evaluating the various advantages to planning, programming, and budgeting, the most promising process which has been developed to date is the trade-off procedure. In a trade-off, the manager looks at an item or a set of items in the budget and considers what else he could do with the same amount of money.

> Rather than replacing two teachers, what could be done with $20,000 which would improve instruction? The per unit of output cost of teaching Latin is $13.80. Is it possible to provide some form of packaged instruction for Latin students at a cost considerably less than the $3,500 expended presently?

The case which is described in the remainder of this chapter was presented by the faculty of a Connecticut school as a proposal to the superintendent of schools. One full-time and two part-time teachers were leaving and the five teams of teachers were presented with the option of expending the $20,000 which it would cost to hire replacements for some other purpose. Since the school was organized in clusters of 120 children there was considerable flexibility in pupil teacher assignments. Before the planning was completed, another $5,000 was added to the trade-off proposal. The purpose of the plan was to improve instruction and the rationale is contained in the presentation. The trade-off proposal which was developed is presented here exactly as it went to the superintendent early in 1970. The trade-offs and salaries are those actually used.

A BUDGET TRADE-OFF PROPOSAL

I. A Brief Description of the Proposal

This proposal offers a personnel "trade-off" in which specific personnel expenditures presented in the 1970-1971 school budget will be "traded-off" for other personnel and materials. A five year plan is projected with current average salaries and prorata expenditures employed for the purpose of tying the "trade-off" base to changes which occur in each of the five years.

II. Rationale

The purposes of this proposal are:
A. To improve instruction:

    . . . by assigning non-teaching, tutorial, and training functions to paraprofessionals.

    . . . by improving the effectiveness of instructional aides through training and incentives, thus differentiating between instructional aides who can instruct under teacher supervision, and clerical aides.

    . . . by individualizing instruction through purchasing materials and equipment which have not been made available in our regular budget.

B. To elevate the status of the staff teacher:

    . . . by relieving teachers of non-teaching, tutorial, and training functions.

    . . . by decreasing the number of teachers needed to support the student enrollment, thereby making it easier for a community to provide an equitable professional salary.

    . . . by increasing the teachers' involvement with high level teaching, including such functions as seminar leader, master presenter, coordinator of independent study, and group counselor.

C. To improve the professional in-service program of the school . . . . .

    . . . by appointing resource teachers to maintain new programs and pilot project teachers to introduce programs which are considered desirable. (This provision has not been included in this year's trade-off.)

    . . . by clearly establishing the job description of resource teacher, pilot project teacher, instructional aide, and clerical aide so that role expectations are clarified and improvement is related to objectives. (The clarification of roles and upgrading of positions would occur through in-service training.)

III. Proposal

We would like to "trade-off" the following budgeted items:

1	classroom teacher (to replace Mrs._____)	
	@ current avr.	$10,000
2	part-time teachers @ current avr.	10,000
2/3	substitute-teacher allotment: (our prorata allotment of $21,000 would be 31 of 216 teachers, roughly 1/7. 1/7 x $21,000 = 3,000.) 2/3 x $3,000 =	2,000

1/4 differentiated staffing allotment. 1/4 x 4,000 =		1,000
1	library clerk	1,050
1	clerk	1,600
		25,650

We would like to buy the following:

3 clerical aides @ $2,520.	$ 7,560
2 instructional aide differentials (20% of clerical aide base)	1,315
1 teacher intern (permanent substitute, substitute teacher coordinator, library clerk, clerk)	6,000

Instructional equipment and materials –	
Cluster E	4,492
Cluster D	2,500
Cluster C	2,500
	$24,367

5% return to school budget	$ 1,283

IV. Five Year Plan

This proposal is offered as a five year plan with the following provisions:

1. Teachers eliminated would be credited at the average teacher salary for the calendar year in question.
2. Prorata figures for substitute teachers and differentiated staffing funds will be adjusted to each year's actual budget figures.
3. Trade-offs of other personnel such as a library clerk will be based on each year's actual budget figures.
4. All new personnel would be brought in at salaries equivalent to current year budget figures.

V. Summary

Eliminated:

1 full-time teacher	$10,000
2 part-time teachers	10,000
1 library clerk	1,050
1 clerk	1,600
2/3 substitute teacher allotment	2,000

Added:
3 clerical aides	$7,560
2 differential (20%) for instructional aides	1,315
1 teacher intern	6,000
equipment and materials for individualized instruction	9,492

VI. Five Year Projection

The present trade-off procedure is projected to year two (Y2) based on a 5 percent increase in all salary items. In year three (1973-1974—Y3) an additional teacher will be traded-off for two instructional aides. Beginning with year three, the return to the town budget will be 10 percent.

TRADE-OFF:

	1970-1971	Y2	Y3	Y4	Y5
Salaries	25,650	28,200	41,000	43,000	45,000

BUY:

	1970-1971	Y2	Y3	Y4	Y5
Salaries	14,875	15,600	24,500	25,900	27,200
Non-Sal.	9,492	11,200	12,200	12,800	13,300
Return	1,283	1,400	4,100	4,300	4,500
	25,650	28,200	41,000	43,000	45,000

SUMMARY

Program budgets:
... Set up trade-offs of one output for another.
... Provide a rationale for distributing resources.
... Predict future income and expenditures.

. . . Relate input to output.

. . . Relate output to policy.

. . . Compare the cost/benefits of alternatives.

. . . Provide continuous feedback for program and project review and revision.

EIGHT

Avoiding the "Systems Trap"

A systems approach is neutral only as long as it isn't being used. The moment someone begins to analyze, design, or operate a system, the biases and values of the systems engineer come into play. As school administrators, we must be aware not only of how systems operate but also how "operators" use systems. This chapter will be devoted to a consideration of some of the unfortunate consequences which will result if school administrators are not alert to the traps and pitfalls along the way. Effectiveness and efficiency are the keynotes of a systems approach. When things which are bad for education are done effectively and efficiently, we are in for trouble. The purpose of this chapter is to point out the dangers in store for those who do not critically examine what they are getting into.

On the other side of the coin, there is the advantage in a questionable systems approach that it expedites honest inquiry. The purpose and process of the operation should be available to anyone who takes the time to investigate. We will take advantage of this situation throughout this chapter.

LET THE BUYER BEWARE!

Avoiding the Mystique of "In Terms"

Various organizations are quick to take advantage of current "in" terms. "A systems approach," "accountability," "cost effectiveness," and "performance objectives" are all phrases which help to sell programs. Unfortunately, in many instances these phrases have no relationship to the instructional materials they are supposed to describe.

It is up to school administrators to identify the improper claims of those who profit from sales to schools. Ideally, professional associations should take a firm stand on false labeling by publishing the names of firms which continue to misrepresent their wares after being warned. Until this happens each individual administrator will have to protect his clients from harm by being knowlegeable and by investigating before purchasing.

"Cost-effectiveness"

Some firms are moving quickly at this time to join the cost-effectiveness bandwagon. "No learning—no money" is the slogan of the day. The intent of such endeavors is commendable but the procedures which are used do not even deal with cost-effectiveness. Effectiveness, as we learned in Chapter One, is judged in terms of a close fit between goals and outcome. When goals are equated with a company's materials, and outcome is measured by normative testing, where is effectiveness? This term can only be applied when the criterion standard which will represent goal attainment is measured and this means that program objectives and performance objectives must be stated.

The very process of buying someone's materials to test effectiveness or efficiency does not make sense in a systems approach. What these organizations should be saying to us is, "Our materials can better accomplish what *you* are trying to do and at less cost, than other materials available to you." At that point we could refer to *our own* performance objectives and say, "Prove it!"

"Accountability"

We all like to think that we are accountable for what we do. We might even agree to be held accountable. In truth, accountability is a rather hollow word. Accountable for doing what? How well? For whom? On what terms?

Any firm which sells its wares on the basis of accountability and then offers standardized normative testing as proof is guilty of perpetuating the myth that these tests measure our objectives. And what of the dilemma that is provided for the poor administrator? Either select an easy test so the results will look good, and pay your money, or select a difficult test in order to assure more rebates, and look bad.

One company which specializes in sophisticated electronic equipment uses very large lettering to advertise accountability. This firm charges each student $1.50 per hour of instruction. For this money the school is able to rent the sophisticated equipment but uses its own staff. As for accountability, this firm promises to rebate ten cents per hour for each month below grade level the student scores on a standardized test of the school's choice. If the student makes no gain at all, proving that the materials were worthless for him, his school is rebated $1.00 per hour. What is not stated is that the firm has earned $.50 per student hour for having done nothing! The public needs to be protected from this kind of accountability.

"Performance Objectives Sold Here"

Some companies offer performance objectives with their programs as an incentive to buy. Anyone who has read this far should be able to tell in short order whether the objects in question deserve to be called performance objectives. What is really in question is why anyone should be stipulating objectives for the schools. It is legitimate and advisable for organizations to state in performance terms *what they are trying to accomplish,* but in the final analysis, school administrators must select their own objectives and then seek materials which promise to satisfy them.

The Flow Chart Mystique

One of the quickest ways to convince the unwary that one knows what systems are all about is to throw a few flow charts into the act. We have seen that flow charts serve the function of being conceptualized models of interrelationships. No one can deny that a good flow chart is worth a thousand words. What the school administrator must guard against is allowing inappropriate flow charts to relay the impression that a system has been conceived.

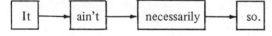

Stacking the Deck

There is something very convincing and final about a systems report. Somehow it conveys the impression that there is nothing more to be said on the subject, but this attitude would be both dangerous and irresponsible. When considering the merits of a program which purports to be the result of a thorough systems approach, it is possible to get to the heart of the matter immediately. When misrepresenters use systems, they usually stack the deck in their favor in one of a few key spots: in the statement of performance objectives, in the presentation of alternatives, or in the report of cost/benefits.

HIHO Programs

There are many HIHO programs on the market. They should be easy to recognize because they don't really accomplish very much. The one thing they do have is an elegant systems format. In fact, the format may be technically perfect. There are impressive PERT schedules and concise flow charts. They can pass tests of effectiveness and efficiency with flying colors. There is only one thing wrong with these programs—the objectives which they attain aren't worth all the bother. Hence, the name HIHO: hokum in—hokum out.

Self-fulfilling Objectives

The objective which motivated the first vivisectionists was to verify Aveccina. The objective of any investigation should be to discover truth. Rather than to report only those discoveries which support the bias, an honest investigation reports all the findings, pro or con. The bind that the investigators were caught up in was that their objective restricted their purpose to verifying that what Aveccina had to say about the anatomy of the body was indeed true. Rather than modify the theory to fit the facts, the facts were forced to verify the theory. This is the nature of a self-fulfilling objective; it has no choice but to verify itself.

Many enabling objectives succumb to the same narrow point of view. At one time, they justified their existence as means to ends, but output measures were always related to the objective and never to the goal. When diagraming sentences was selected as an enabling objective for the goal of improving written and oral communication, the assumption was implicit that diagraming had something to do with attaining a major goal of society—improving the ability to communicate. In measuring the objective the deck was stacked. The criterion measure was how well youngsters could diagram sentences rather than how well they could write and speak. If evaluation is not relevant to higher level goals or terminal objectives, the measurement program verifies the objective rather than testing it. This is the way in which self-fulfilling objectives are born. It should not be difficult for the reader to think of further examples. *Any program which evaluates the method rather than the terminal objective severs its relationship with the systems approach.*

Pot-and-Kettle Alternatives

Five of the tasks outlined in Chapter One dealt with alternatives. At these critical points the analysts, the designers, and the operators bring options to the manager in order that he can make a decision. These alternatives should be the best available. They should represent both convergent and divergent thinking. Some should emphasize effectiveness and others, efficiency. If all of the alternatives presented cluster around one point of view, the manager is not really given the most important option. When the analyst selects the process and the manager chooses between pots and kettles, the system has been turned upside down.

Cost/Benefit Jazz

Cost/benefit is a concept that has wide appeal. Everyone believes in it. The only problem is that while school administrators are deciding how to utilize cost/benefit to improve instruction, some producers of educational materials are presenting their own version of cost/benefit to the public. The only meaningful figure which the producers can contribute is *cost.* Cost efficiency, or low cost because of efficient methods, can only be proven in action. Cost effectiveness, or attaining objectives at the lowest cost, is meaningful only from the viewpoint of the school system. We already know what cost/benefit means to the producers—**profit.**

The concept of cost/benefit is a decision-making tool. Its purpose is to help managers make good choices. Producers provide costs and performance specifications and school administrators figure cost/benefits. In this way, the entire procedure will be kept very business-like. Rather than saying, "You can use what we make," the firms will have to say, "We can make what you want to use." The difference is crucial to the determination of who makes the policy decisions in education.

THE BUILT-IN BIAS FOR TRADITION

The aspect of systems approaches which deserves the closest attention from educators is that a systems approach has a built-in bias for a traditional form of education. Some of the reasons for this are obvious. Others are subtle and bear constant watching. In this section we will examine the ways in which traditional methods are favored, and some of the difficulties which divergent programs will have to overcome.

Traditional Objectives Are Easy to Validate

Both traditional and progressive education pursue essentially the same goals and terminal objectives, but their basic philosophical premises indicate quite different enabling objectives. Traditional education favors a broad accumulation of knowledge and therefore tests for low cognitive retention. Progressive education prefers higher cognitive involvement, and affective outcomes. It is much easier to validate the objectives of traditional education because the expected performance can be very precisely described. An additional advantage is that education has been providing a model for the methods and measures of traditional instruction for centuries. Even teachers who are instinctively progressive have no models for validating what they are doing. The very graduate courses which have turned them in this direction often resort to low cognitive measurement.

When objectives are directed toward higher cognition and affective outcomes, validation is more difficult. Bloom and Krathwohl[1] have helped immeasurably but even their efforts indicate how much more complex the task is.

Under ordinary circumstances this would not be a serious problem because teachers would continue doing what they believed in without being too concerned about measurement. The systems approach forces the issue. Objectives have to be stated in performance terms and measurement is directed to this criterion. There is a real danger that if rewards and punishments for teachers are based on measurement of performance, the tendency will be to fall back on the more certain world of facts and skills.

There is also a danger that administrative regulations will be plugged in which prescribe process goals which are more conservative than those we know. "Conditioned response" is as much a process as is "discovery." In a systems approach, these high level directives would be much more difficult to ignore than they would be under present circumstances.

There is no doubt that any system which emphasizes validation will present difficulties for those programs which are concerned with synthesis and evaluation of knowledge and an internalization of affective goals. Some possibilities for dealing with this situation will be presented in the section, "Avoiding the Trap."

---

[1] Bloom, *Taxonomy of Education Objectives.*

Normative Testing Rewards Status Quo

Normative testing, the familiar national standardized tests, have only limited use in a systems approach. We desperately need tests which are a head-on measure of what we are trying to do. Criterion measures, a direct measurement of the fit between the criterion stated in the objective and the output, are ideally suited to systems purposes. Why is it so difficult to get the kind of testing which is needed?

In the first place, there is a great deal of mystification surrounding normative tests. They have the reputation of being "hard data" because of their widespread use in research. There is no good reason why tests which are suitable for research purposes should also be good for criterion evaluation. Normative tests are designed to spread scores out on a statistical curve. The test must have a high ceiling in order to distribute the top 50 percent along a slope which is equivalent to the lower half. In order for this to happen, there must be a number of test items which represent material which has not been taught. By definition, there must be a good share of items which the average student will not be able to answer correctly.

Another reason why normative tests persist is that they are available and criterion tests are not. The testing companies do not produce criterion tests and few school systems have the necessary staff to develop their own.

A third reason, one that is difficult to understand, is that normative tests are felt to represent "standards." The hard line accountability proponents feel that they have a measure of performance in normative testing. Look at the facts. If you support normative testing, you begin with the premise that a certain percent of the group will fail *no matter what the nature of the group might be.* It is difficult to see what is so hard line about this. The basic premise of criterion testing is that *everyone is expected to meet the standard.*

A school system which is venturing into new areas would much rather test itself on what it is attempting to do than on what a normative test expects of the average performer. An example of the testing dilemma can be seen in the case of schools which are using Cuisenaire rods for teaching mathematics. In this program, children in the first year of school are learning all mathematical operations simultaneously. They can multiply, divide, factor, and operate with fractions. Traditional tests do not even measure these operations. The Cuisenaire youngster has to compete in a narrow segment of his preparation with children who spend full time on these limited operations.

School administrators must resist the efforts of state and federal officials to prescribe normative testing as evidence of performance. These tests do not validate anything specifically. They are not hard data—in fact, they are rather mushy. They tend to support the status quo at the expense of progressive change. They are not consistent with the concept of criterion measurement which is necessary in a systems approach. *They do not even set up a standard.*

The Better Housekeeping Cult

Many systems engineers become so mesmerized by the sheer elegance of a neat system that no one is allowed to mess things up by suggesting that the objectives are no longer meaningful. The objectives can be stated according to Mager's criteria, the methods and means of attaining the objectives can be 100 percent effective, efficiency ratings can be nearly perfect, and yet the program can still be worthless. Any system that is so intent on operating smoothly that it never asks itself important existential questions isn't really a good system.

A preoccupation with housekeeping works against progressive change. *In order for change to be meaningful, it must pose serious questions directed at the objectives.* If the objectives are vulnerable, the entire system will probably have to be changed. Now that we have seen the complex interrelationships that combine to form a system, it is easy to see why the major task of a system is to preserve its function. This is supportive of current practice, but bad news for innovative programs.

AVOIDING THE TRAP

It is possible to avoid all of the traps and biases that were mentioned in the first two sections of this chapter. It could be pointed out that every one of these pitfalls would be avoided if the system were properly operated.

With all of this built-in protection there are still several safeguards which should be taken. This section will describe some procedures for avoiding the more common pitfalls.

Developing a Broad Base for Evaluation

When you can't validate—postulate! Probably the number one constraint which stands in the way of a more widespread acceptance of systems analysis is the difficulty in validating higher cognitive and affective outcomes. Traditionalists point to this as proof of a basic weakness in progressive programs. Progressives, unable to answer, shrug and maintain that they aren't in favor of dehumanizing measurement approaches anyway. As a result, systems approaches are more often introduced by mandate than by common agreement which is most unfortunate. There is no need for validation to be a constraint.

The first concern of the instructional designer should not be to validate his theory but to *postulate* it. The performance objectives which result will still have to be stated in behavioral terms. When objectives are explicit as to anticipated change in behavior, they are open to honest inquiry. Proponents can evaluate to prove and opponents can test to condemn. *Postulation will force validation.* It is only necessary to find the method of evaluation.

Critics will object that it is not good systems practice to operate the system before validation procedures have been confirmed. This is true. The point made here is that unrealistic preoccupation with validation results in a stalemate. Postulating what is expected to occur will make it easier to design ways of evaluating the results.

Evaluation is more than measurement. "Evaluation is something more than measurement," implies that measurement is a special kind of evaluation and that there are other kinds. The appropriate concern in a systems approach is evaluation, for this admits as evidence any indication of behavioral change. Measurement is concerned with a number scale rating of objective attainment. Evaluation is concerned with growth and change, however it can be detected or described.

The point made here is that there are many legitimate ways to evaluate other than number scale measurement. The products which are produced by students can be assessed, learning processes can be judged, and behavior can be described. In all cases, qualitative judgments are admissible. It is not necessary to restrict thinking to measurement tests in order to satisfy the requirements of validation. It may even be that a metric scale does not apply to certain behavioral changes and that proper evaluation will await further development of Kurt Lewin's topological approach to the description of behavior.[2]

Elegant quantification and relevant qualification. Most educators have been conditioned to equate validation with quantification. Research scholars have had a stranglehold on evaluation in education for many

---

[2] Kurt Lewin, *Principles of Topological Psychology.* (New York: McGraw-Hill Book Company, 1936).

years. Research has a different function from on-going evaluation and, in fact, is a process which is antithetical to evaluation in many ways. Research demands highly controlled conditions and statistical validation. The on-going educational program cannot allow itself to be controlled by the rigid restrictions which research demands. Research is ex post facto analysis in a laboratory situation. Evaluation is here-and-now analysis in the classroom.

It is probably because of our own educational background that we have permitted research design to be substituted for evaluation procedures for all these years. We should keep in mind that the researcher is interested in discovering principles about relationships in learning. The collection of relevant data and the control of variables mark his approach. The evaluator is concerned with making decisions on the spot. He needs to discover what is most feasible. He needs tools which help him to select the best alternative.

Elegant quantification is the best form of validation when it is appropriate because people are convinced by measurements which appear to be both relative and absolute. Relevant qualification will have to be accepted in areas where quantification is not appropriate and measurement is an exercise in hokum. Statistical decision theory, game theory, and information theory are new management devices which are largely qualitative judgments with an overlay of measurement. The Delphi approach, approval by consensus, group decision-making, and intuitive choice are qualitative judgments which, as long as they remain relevant, can serve to validate instructional progress.

Analyzing the Objectives

The most crucial task which faces management in the process of adopting someone else's system is to scrutinize the objectives. Evaluation has answered the question, "Are the objectives which are stated attained?" An even more important question is, "Are the objectives which are stated worth attaining?" It is inexcusable for a school administrator to buy objectives on faith. Usually this is done based on an intuitive feeling that the philosophy of a program corresponds to one's own philosophy. Once objectives are stated, they become the embodiment of a philosophy and for all practical purposes they replace epistomological theory since they become the means of attaining the goals.

The purpose of this analysis of objectives is to provide a practical procedure for checking things out. It is up to the school administrator to determine and preserve his own philosophy. The approach taken here is to provide guidelines for making certain that the system is responsive to whatever this philosophy might be.

Task 1. Identify the hierarchial level. It is necessary to identify the hierarchical level of each set of objectives under consideration. Considerable attention has been given to this process throughout this book so there is no need to repeat the procedure here. All that is necessary is to be able to say with certainty, "These are performance objectives," or "These are program objectives," or "These are goals."

Task 2. Relate objectives to a higher purpose. Objectives must be responsive to higher objectives and eventually to goals. This is a chain of relevance directed toward a goal and all links of the chain must be there. Non-responsive low order objectives are an exercise in folly. It is necessary to identify the higher purpose objectives and goals in the program, or to indicate one's own higher purpose objectives and goals to which the objectives in question relate.

Task 3. Assess the relevancy of the objectives. This is the single most important task to be performed by a school administrator in evaluating a program for adoption. With the program's objectives identified (Task 1) and the chain of higher objectives established (Task 2), it is now possible to assess the objectives in terms of their relevancy to one's own purpose. This must be done for both the structure and the process of the system.

Structure is a conceptualization of all of the interrelationships which constitute a system. It is the structure which provides the strength of organization. There are several things to check out at this point:

1. If the program under consideration has a stated structure is it compatible with whatever structure has been conceived for the organization's purpose?
2. If the program under consideration has no stated structure, determine what the structure is and compare it to your own conceptualization.
3. Are the stated objectives related to the proposed structure in such a way that they are responsive to the structure and utilize it as a framework for understanding the purpose of the operation? (Example: If the structure of a unit of study on the Inca's is "concepts about early cultures," the objectives should indicate that the desired performance of the learner is directed to these same concepts. If, instead, the objectives stressed the acquisition of facts, the structure, however well postulated, would not be transmitted to the learner.)

Whatever methods and means are indicated in the objectives must also be related to the desired process goals. If one believes with Suchman that the inquiry process is vital to learning, it would be important to check out the methods and means indicated in the objectives to determine their orientation relative to inquiry. If, on the other hand, one agrees with Ausubel that youngsters who are able to deal with abstractions should spend most of their time learning from didactic presentations, it would be necessary to investigate the objectives to see if they were oriented to didactic learning.

The methods and means which are stated in enabling objectives should never be permitted to become ends in themselves. This danger was indicated in the previous section as "self-fulfilling objectives." We have already seen how evaluation can be used to test the relevancy of objectives to higher objectives. When we are considering the objectives, the question becomes, "What is the relation between the attainment of this enabling objective and the attainment of the terminal objective to which it is directed?" Some may consider this to be so self-evident that no warning is necessary. If educators had been asking this question down through the years, countless generations of children would have been spared diagramming sentences, spelling lists, reciprocal rules for dividing fractions, geometric theorems, grammar, Latin, and numerous other vestiges of a former era when rigorous activities were considered to be exercises for the brain.

HUMANIZING THE SYSTEM

A systems approach is a tool for decision making which enables the person who manages the system to state his bias in the form of a goal, and to operate the system so that performance is checked to be certain that the bias is being attained. Too often, the systems approach is termed inhumane, or de-personalized. The system will be inhumane or impersonal if that is the bias which established its purpose. On the other hand, *if the purpose of the system is to promote humane interests, the output should be an effective and efficient humanized system.* This section will be devoted to a complete analysis of a systems approach in order to indicate the many ways in which humane outcomes can be postulated and produced. In so doing, it must be acknowledged that our bias is to create a humane system. Systems can be either inhumane and de-personalized or personalized and humane. They will be whatever they are designed to be.

Formulating Humane Process Goals

We declare the purpose of a system in the statement of goals. The goals describe the outcome which is desired in terms of the product which is being produced or the process of production. *When humans are among the inputs to the system, the process must recognize their humanity by being humane.* We can guarantee that the operations of the system will never lose sight of this obligation by postulating these commitments in the form of process goals. Process goals reflect the bias of society and the organizations of society concerning *how* the system operates. Since our bias has been revealed as a strong preference for methods and means which respect the dignity of each individual human being in a manner which permits no person to be the means to another person's ends, our process goals should reflect that bias. Here are some illustrations:

> The public schools should:
>
> I.B. Develop programs which help young people to accept responsibility for self-evaluation and continuing self-instruction.
>
> VI.A. Provide the opportunity for each student to proceed at his own pace in instructional programs geared to his personal needs.
>
> IV.B. Develop a school atmosphere which promotes mutual respect and responsible behavior.
>
> V.A. Treat each youngster with respect for his human dignity.

When humane intentions are expressed as process goals, there is a high level commitment which should give direction to administrative regulations, objectives, methods and means, operations, and evaluation.

Developing Humane Objectives and Regulations

When goals are directed to process, the performance specifications of objectives and regulations refer to *how* things are to happen rather than *what* the outcome is expected to be. We will trace organizational goal I.B and develop a program objective, a performance objective, and regulations to support each level.

Organizational Goal I.B.
The public schools should develop programs which help young people to accept responsibility for self-evaluation and continuing self-instruction under the guidance of a teacher.

Administrative Regulation I.B.
Each school should organize its instructional programs in such a way that instruments for self-evaluation are readily available. Self-instruction should be encouraged by providing clear objectives for learners so that they can select materials and content which are appropriate for their personal needs. Referral to a teacher or tutor at regular intervals, especially

when difficulties are experienced, should be built into the procedure and
not left to chance.

Program Objective I.B.1

Each student should be able to use the unit mastery tests for Algebra II
any time that he chooses, and the results are for his own assessment and
not for the teacher's rating.

Each student should find it possible to obtain self-instructional materials for skills review, continuous progress in the base program, and concept enrichment. Referral to the teacher or tutor should be automatic and
problems should be detected, evaluated, and presented to the teacher as
they occur.

Administrative Regulation I.B.1

Each school should provide and maintain a complete battery of self--
evaluation tests for Algebra II.

Each school should make available to students on a prescriptive or
contractual basis self-instructional materials for skills review, continuous
progress, and concept enrichment.

Provisions should be made for automatic detection, evaluation, and
immediate referral to the teacher.

Performance Objective I.B.1a

Each student should be able to interpret prescription and contract
sheets and select the self-instructional and self-evaluation material indicated for the appropriate map and globe unit. He should know how to
utilize the assistance of the teacher or tutors.

Administrative Regulation I.B.1a

Each school should make available self-instructional materials on map
and globe skills which include pre-tests, prescription and contract sheets,
teacher referral, self-evaluation tests, mastery tests and post-tests.

Selecting Alternatives for Humane Considerations

When the priority in a systems operation is cost/benefit, there is a
danger that production might be considered more important than human
welfare. One of the specific instructions to the analysts and designers who
work on the system should direct them to consider humane factors. In
Chapter One, specific directions were outlined which emphasized a consideration for the humans who would be affected.

Task: Consider the goal alternatives

Is the goal completely responsive to the desires of those who will be
affected?

Task: Identify the performance alternatives

Are there humane factors which would make alternative procedures
more desirable even though somewhat less productive?

Task: Identify the alternative components
Are the methods and means selected for attaining the objectives considerate of human welfare?

Maintaining Humanized Commitments Through Evaluation

Evaluation serves the function of maintaining the purpose of the system through detection and correction of deviations. When humane purposes have been established, it is possible to monitor them so that they remain responsive to the process goals from which they originated.

Usually process goals are evaluated during the operation of a system rather than at the output. If a process commitment has been made to treat each young person with respect for his human dignity, this can be most effectively evaluated in process.

Is it possible to evaluate the instructional process as objectively as the products of instruction? If the product is a low level cognitive goal, the answer is no. However, it is no more difficult than evaluating higher level outcomes in the cognitive and affective domains for the same type of assessment procedures are used.

Essentially, the function which must be performed by evaluation of the instructional process is to determine whether or not the desired process of instruction is the actual process. Traditional observation procedures have no contribution to make but there are new techniques available which show promise.

Microteaching and similar techniques which incorporate video-tape playback show a great deal of potential. When process goals are clearly understood and the teacher and supervisor work cooperatively to attain the necessary tactics, these are essentially self-evaluation techniques. It would seem that when a change in teacher behavior is needed in order to produce a new method of teaching that nothing would work quite as rapidly as microteaching incorporating a demonstration of desired techniques, an effort by the teacher to achieve the same effect, a self-evaluation by the teacher of her teaching via video-tape replay, an evaluation of the same episode by other observers including students, an offer of suggestions for consideration, and then another cycle with changes incorporated. This type of an evaluation of microteaching is mostly intuitive with little hard data backing at this time, but as we learn more about the ways to evaluate changes in behavior it seems likely that methods of this type will score high.

Interaction analysis is another technique of considerable promise. Observers in a classroom classify what is happening into ten types of activities. Every three seconds a checkmark indicates which activity is taking place. It is possible to indicate that there is teacher talk, student talk, or silence. Teacher talk can be indirect or direct. When these results are charted, it would be possible to analyze them with reference to the process goal desired. It would be possible to construct an interaction analysis which was directed to the specific process in question. If, for example, an attempt was being made to evaluate the extent to which students were treated with respect and in turn behaved respectfully, an analysis of all of the indicators of mutual respect would be a necessary prerequisite.

Classroom analysis is a scheme for transcribing what is being said or done and making appropriate annotations in the form of a running commentary. This procedure, like microteaching, does not lend itself to reliable quantification, but it shows considerable promise for bringing about change in teacher behavior.

One last technique deserves attention: the anthropological field study. In this technique, the observer spends a great deal of time in the classroom and reacts to what he sees. The results are most impressive when the observer is sensitive, knows what he is looking for, and does not have a preconceived idea about what should be happening. John Holt's observations in the classroom are of this nature even though he did not knowingly employ this method. He merely paid careful attention to what was really happening and recorded the difference between objectives and reality. They were considerable.

Creating Time for Humanizing

Perhaps the greatest benefit to be derived from a systems approach is that it can create time for humanizing experiences. If all of the learning which now occurs in a school day could be compressed into a smaller time block, the time which is left over could be utilized for creativity, enrichment, guidance, and exploration. These are high level humanizing experiences which we would claim are occurring in our schools now, but how much time is really devoted to these endeavors? We are so pressured and preoccupied with basic skills, content coverage, and textbooks that most of the school day is invested in these activities. What if it were possible to accomplish all of these things just as effectively and much more efficiently?

This is not to suggest that the day should be separated into systems and non-systems segments. Neither is it intended to delegate to a systems approach the low level functions of education with the implication that it is not appropriate for more creative ventures. In the concluding section of this chapter, the opposite thesis will be pursued. What is maintained is that those who fear the dehumanizing effects of a systems approach have no cause for alarm. The following assertions may help to allay these concerns:

1. A system can be programmed to be humanizing. In this case, the goals, methods and means, and evaluation program will all be synchronized to one purpose—an effective and efficient humane system.
2. We must deal with the myth that what is now happening in the schools is humanizing. If intimate contact with a wise empathetic instructor is important, how much of this is actually occurring in a traditional classroom? Interaction analysis studies indicate that this personal contact just does not occur that often. One of the process goals of a system might be to provide more intimacy between students and adults using the same amount of money now budgeted for staff.
3. A systems approach does not de-personalize education unless it is designed sepcifically for that purpose.
4. A systems approach is neither for nor against ecstasy in education. If this happens to be the bias of the designer of the system, however, it will attain whatever form of ecstasy one can describe.
5. The capability of a systems approach to achieve its goals efficiently could provide the time which is needed for a humane education by achieving skills and content objectives in much less time.

EDUCATION IN 2001 A.D.

A look into the future is a fantasy which systems advocates enjoy. It is not too difficult to conjure up elegantly engineered electronics because the capability for producing exotic wares is already at hand. There will be no mention of hardware here. The instructional equipment now available will do nicely for 2001 A.D.

The problem with education in the early 1970's is that the expertise of technology has been restricted to the media aspect of education when the real need had been a complete new conceptualization of instruction as a system. What is required is a systems approach to learning theory.

The following definitions of various instructional media are intended to indicate the source of the problem:

Instructional Films — A two channel presentation of content which would be boring enough on either one alone.

Educational Television — A sophisticated research study which should prove for all time that no one likes a thirty-minute lecture.

Programmed Instruction— Take one textbook and break it down into minute sequential steps and you get one dull self-paced learning program.

If the systems approach has a contribution to make which will make the education of the year 2001 A.D. something far more exciting than what we now have, this contribution will have to be in the area of instructional systems and not media. We will consider how this might happen.

A Systems Theory of Learning Will Be Available

Until all of the theories of learning are systhesized and brought together in one system, there will be no effective way of unifying the structure and process of instruction and the ability and needs of the learner. In Chapter Five we discovered that it was impossible to design an individualized unit of instruction until a theoretical unit of instruction was conceptualized. An attempt was made to relate a conceptual structure with presentational modes and learner attributes. There is room for a great deal of theorizing and experimenting in this area.

A systems theory of learning is a high priority need as the initial step to be taken in paving the way for instructional programs of 2001. At the present time, instruction has its most visible structure in the form of the content of instructional materials. The structure of English 5 in most communities is an English 5 textbook. Where a course of study is available, it is probably based on a skills sequence and an allotment of topics such as, "writing a business letter."

In Chapter Five it was proposed that a hierarchical ordering of objectives is the most logical structure for education. Once objectives are put in order, the major concepts of each objective can be used to develop another dimension to this structure.

Somehow structure, process, presentational mode, and content have to be matched with the attributes of the learner. One way in which this might be done was proposed in Figure 16. There are a number of other possibilities. In any event, what is clearly needed is a fully developed theory of instruction where instruction is viewed as a total system and all of the major interrelationships are brought together in one organic unit.

Instructional Units in 2001 A.D.

In 2001, instructional units will be much more flexible than any now available. Each unit will indicate *what* has to be accomplished and the teacher will function as a strategist in selecting the most appropriate options for the individual learner. With decisions to be made concerning the presentational form and the content desired, the learner will also be active in designing the final package.

Obviously, instructional units of the type described could be designed at this time. The unit developed in Chapter Five followed this format. The problem is that most commercial materials are geared to content partitioned in topics and usually packaged in yearly portions. There will be an interlude when we have to make the best match possible between our objectives and the content of commercial materials. Eventually there will be instructional units which indicate the objectives and concepts, leaving it to the teacher and student to work out a contractual agreement concerning the presentational mode, the content, and the media.

Evaluation of Behavioral Change

There is an obvious lag between our readiness to indicate the change in behavior we desire and our ability to determine whether the change has occurred. Beyond low level cognitive behavior, our detectors are not very sensitive. This will have to change. The whole concept of a systems approach is built around the attainment of a prescribed level of performance. It is going to become increasingly difficult to make progress unless indicators of change in behavior can be developed which are sensitive to the complex changes which occur in synthesis, evaluation, and affectivity. It is almost certain that these instruments will be more qualitative than quantitative. It does not seem that interaction analysis, classroom analysis, or microteaching have this potential since they are not related to a mathematical interpretation which is non-linear. At the present time, the mathematical analysis of general systems is best accomplished by topology since it is a qualitative form of mathematics. Perhaps the unfinished work of Kurt Lewin in topological psychology related to behavior can be further developed to meet this challenge. Until this is done, the evaluation of behavioral change in higher cognitive functions will be difficult.

A Unification of All Sciences

The greatest contribution to be made by systems science is the unification of all the sciences, including the social sciences. It is general systems theory which is most suitable to taking on a problem of this dimension. In fact, this is the ultimate goal to which general systems theory is directed. What is intended in the ultimate form is a theoretical or conceptual unification of all of the sciences in such a way that they are related to the same general principles and have a common operational language including a mathematics.

The scope of this venture is certainly beyond the type of systems approach which has been developed in this book. This is not a problem because the general systems theorists are making excellent progress and will probably reach their goal within the next decade. One such proposal, the result of a life-long study by Haskell, has already been written.[3] This massive undertaking has achieved the ultimate goal in impressive fashion.

The implications of a unified science for our school systems are far reaching. The separate disciplines will probably retain their identity, but when they are brought together to solve problems which cross into several fields, the full power of a meta-science will be brought to bear. This will demand new conceptualizations, a unified meta-language, and a new mathematics.

With the advent of a unified science on the horizon, it is important that we have our own house in order. The further along we are in attaining the projects outlined in this section, the better equipped we will be to relate our own operations to whatever new educational structures emerge.

Two Cultures United — 2001 A.D.

In *The Two Cultures,* C.P. Snow presented a brilliant analysis of the separate worlds of the humanists and the scientists. Technology is both scientific and humanistic and therefore is the key to uniting the two cultures. The thrust which has elevated man from one major age to another has been technological advancement—hand tools, artifacts, manufacture, and automation. With each of these advances man has become more civilized and more sensitive to his humanness. While many view the world of today as de-personalized and inhuman, it is more accurate to point out that there is an increased awareness of the need for humanizing our institutions. The systems approach can accelerate the advance toward "the world of one culture."

> In the world of one culture:
> - Goals of society and of organizations will be more viable, more responsive to human desires.
> - Performance objectives will be selected for individual prescriptions. (Depending upon each learner's individual attributes, there are many optional performances for attaining terminal or program objectives.)
> - Criterion measures for creativity, sensitive awareness, humaneness, self-concept, and spirituality will be assessed with confidence.

---

[3] Edward Haskell, *Assembly of the Sciences into a Single Discipline,* (445 Riverside Drive, New York: Copyrighted manuscript, 1968).

- The *quality* of human response will be the major concern of educational goals.
- The sciences, including the social sciences, will be united. (This has already been accomplished in theory by Haskell.)
- Management will be by cybernetic control and evaluation will be topological. (Norbert Weiner and Kurt Lewin have presented the models.)
- Skills training will be accomplished by individual prescription and will be considered to be a *preparation* for education—not education itself.
- Physiological and psychological deterrents to learning will also be treated by individual prescription but this will not be considered to be the educational program for students with these disabilities.
- Self-evaluation, as opposed to individual prescription, will be viewed as a contract between the student and the school.
- Communal education, or learning in groups, will be directed toward improving the quality of human response. Qualitative assessment will be available. (The criterion goal will be established through group inquiry and will be viewed as a change in ethical position rather than as an eternal truth.)
- "The System" will become the solution rather than the problem.

A Commitment to Individualized Instruction

The commitment to individualized instruction in Farmington has been specified in the statement of educational goals, in program objectives, performance objectives, and administrative regulations. These statements are presented here as evidence that the program of individualized instruction in mathematics is responsive to the direction established by the Board of Education in its statement of goals, by the school administration through its regulations, and by the curriculum as stated in program and performance objectives.

Organizational Goal 6.1 Individualized Instruction

The public schools of Farmington shall promote self-realization by helping each child attain the optimum growth and development within his capacity through educational programs which take into account individual differences.

Administrative Regulation 6.1 Individualized Instruction

Each school should be organized to provide maximum opportunity for instruction geared to individual differences. Skills programs should be individually prescribed and study programs should contain provisions for individuals to select materials appropriate for their cognitive level and learning style.

Program Objective 6.1.1 Individualized Instruction

Each course of study should be so designed that individual learners can satisfy their own needs by selecting a form of presentation suitable to their own learning style. All skills programs should be individually prescribed and designed for self-management and regular evaluation of performance. Group experiences and individual experiences should be clearly delineated.

Administrative Regulation 6.1.1a Individualized Instruction

All skills programs in the mathematics department should be organized as soon as possible to provide individual diagnosis and prescription, self-management, and regular feedback of information concerning performance to both the learner and the instructor.

Administrative Regulation 6.1.1b Individualized Instruction

All study programs in the Mathematics department should provide the individual learner with as many options as possible for selecting the presentational mode of instruction. Purpose should be identified with objectives rather than content so that a variety of content will be available for individual selection.

Goals of Society

Suggested Goals for Public Education in Texas[1]

Public education should help each individual to develop to the maximum of his capacity, and to function as a responsible member of a viable, democratic society. Public education in Texas should help each individual to achieve:

1. *Intellectual Discipline.* The schools should:
   - Provide all children with knowledge of the traditionally accepted fundamentals, such as reading, writing and arithmetic in the early elementary grades, accompanied by studies in higher mathematics, science, history and English as they progress through the upper grades.
   - Help each child to develop the power to think constructively, to solve problems, to reason independently, and to accept responsibility for self-evaluation and continuing self-instruction.
   - Help each child gain access to the accumulated culture and knowledge of man.

2. *Economic and Vocational Competence.* The public schools should:
   - Help all students understand how to function effectively in the American economic system.
   - Provide every student with usable vocational skills which will equip him to find employment in the event he finds it impractical to continue his education.
   - Offer guidance and counseling to help every student decide what he should do upon completion of high school.

3. *Citizenship and Civic Responsibility.* The public schools should:
   - Provide for all children citizenship education opportunities and experiences

---

[1] From *Goals for Public Education in Texas,* p. 18.

which emphasize the American heritage and the responsibilities and privileges of citizenship.
— Help equip each child for intelligent participation in the democratic processes through which this country is governed.
— Teach each child to understand the relationship between the United States and other nations of the world.

4. *Competence in Human and Social Relations.* The public schools should:
— Assist each child in his efforts to make a place for himself in the community and to the larger society of the state and nation.
— Help to develop in all children a respect for the rights of others as individuals and as groups, and to understand the requirements that a viable society demands of the individual.

5. *Moral and Ethical Values.* The public schools should:
— Assist in the development of moral and spiritual values, ethical standards of conduct, and basic integrity.

6. *Self-Realization and Mental and Physical Health.* The public schools should:
— Provide educational programs which take into account individual differences.
— Help each child attain the optimum growth and development within his capacity.
— Help each child to attain and preserve physical and mental health, to develop a sense of aesthetic appreciation, and to deal constructively with the psychological tensions inherent in continuing change and adaption.

Administrative Regulations

1. The Farmington Public Schools should develop intellectual discipline.

    1.1 Each youngster should master the fundamental academic skills which are considered to be prerequisite to the acquisition of knowledge. These basic skills should be organized and presented in a manner which makes it possible for each individual learner to progress at his own rate through individually prescribed material. In order to accomplish this goal each school should:

        1.1.1 Determine the major skills which will be taught in each area of the curriculum. (These are to be the end of course skills, not the en-route or means to ends skills.)

        1.1.2 Describe each major skill in performance terms so that it can be determined how the learner must behave in order to evidence mastery of the skill. (This will include a description of the skills, the conditions under which it will be performed, and the standards which will be used to evaluate mastery.)

        1.1.3 Develop a system of evaluation which makes it possible to determine where each learner stands before beginning instruction (pre-test), how each learner is progressing at frequent intervals (mastery test), and how well the end of course standards have been met (post-test).

        1.1.4 Organize a system of instruction which makes it possible for each individual learner to progress through the skills at his own rate.

    1.2 Each youngster should acquire the ability to solve problems and to assume the responsibility for his own education. To assist in achieving this goal each school should:

194

      1.2.1 Institute instructional processes which encourage learning through inquiry and problem solving.

      1.2.2 Develop procedures which make it possible for the learner to establish personal objectives and to evaluate his own progress.

      1.2.3 Develop procedures which make it possible for youngsters to "learn how to learn" so that they can assume the responsibility for their own education.

  1.3   All youngsters should have the opportunity to study and investigate the accumulated culture and knowledge of man. In order to assure that this goal is available each school should:

      1.3.1 Provide the opportunity for youngsters to acquire exemplary study procedures by means of in-depth investigations under teacher guidance.

      1.3.2 Provide the resources and opportunities for youngsters to investigate many areas of knowledge through independent study.

      1.3.3 Organize the curriculum in a manner that emphasizes the structure of each instructional discipline in order to provide organizing power for units of learning.

2.   The Farmington Public Schools should foster economic and vocational competence.

  2.1   Each school should help students to function effectively in the American Economic system:

      2.1.1 By providing real and simulated opportunities for youngsters to experience the realities of contemporary economic life.

      2.1.2 By organizing units of study which emphasize the structure and discipline of economics so that the learner can understand the principles which govern economics.

  2.2   Each school should fulfill its obligation to provide usable vocational skills:

      2.2.1 By promoting skills which emphasize general and universal vocational skills rather than specific skills which may become obsolete.

      2.2.2 By developing work habits and disciplined activity in connection with school work which contribute to an effective attitude toward work.

  2.3   In addition the high school should offer guidance and counseling designed to help each student make a realistic vocational choice.

3.   The Farmington Public Schools should encourage citizenship and civic responsibility.

  3.1   Each school should provide experiences which emphasize the American heritage and the responsibilities and privileges of citizenship.

      3.1.1 Provide opportunities for students to investigate the principles upon which our democratic society was established.

3.1.2 Consider the school to be a democratic society where both the privileges and responsibilities of citizenship are experienced.

3.2 Each school should help prepare each child for intelligent participation in a democratic society.

3.2.1 Organize the school as a democratic society in which the students have many opportunities to discuss the problems of the school community and the relevance of their education.

3.3 Each school should teach each child to understand the relationship between the United States and other nations of the world.

3.3.1 Provide opportunities for students to investigate the economic, governmental, and cultural relationship between our country and various other nations.

4. The Farmington Public Schools should develop competence in human and social relations.

4.1 Each child needs to be assisted in making his place in the community and larger societies. Each school should:

4.1.1 Assist each student to make his place in the school community.

4.1.2 Provide opportunities for students to relate their studies to the real problems of living in their local community.

4.1.3 Help students to understand that their state and nation are human systems which must be responsive to the concerns and needs of people.

4.2 Each student should respect the rights of others and understand his responsibility to society.

4.2.1 Provide real and simulated experiences in which students can make ethical decisions about their rights and responsibilities.

4.2.2 Consider the school to be a viable society in which each individual must understand the requirements that the school places on individuals.

5. The Farmington Public Schools should foster moral and ethical values.

5.1 It is the responsibility of the school to foster moral and spiritual values, ethical conduct, and basic integrity.

5.1.1 Provide regular real and simulated experiences in which students make ethical decisions concerning human behavior. The position of the school will be non-judgmental concerning the discussion of ethical decision making.

5.1.2 The adult staff members of the school should demonstrate exemplary ethical conduct and basic integrity.

5.2 Each school should help each student to develop life goals.

5.2.1 To offset the devastating effect of existential quandry, each school should help its students discover the meaning of their existence through discussions, and meaningful experiences directed toward active involvement in living.

6. The Farmington Public Schools should promote self-realization and mental and physical health.

    6.1   Each school should assist students to explore their own unique potential.

        6.1.1 The organization of the school should provide maximum opportunity for instruction geared to individual differences.

        6.1.2 The instructional process should encourage divergent thinking and creative effort.

    6.2   Each school should help each student attain and preserve physical and mental health.

        6.2.1 Provide frequent opportunities for physical activity.

        6.2.2 Establish health programs which provide information about physical and mental well-being.

        6.2.3 Provide programs in behavior modification for youngsters whose psychological needs interfere with mental health.

    6.3   Each school should exhibit a concern for the development of a positive self-concept.

        6.3.1 Provide a program which makes it possible to detect the detrimental effect of a poor self-concept on school achievement.

        6.3.2 Establish a school climate which offers maximum opportunity for the development of a positive self-concept.

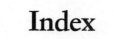
Index

Index